Up From the Ashes

by

ANDI COOK

The views expressed in this book are those of Andi Cook, and do not necessarily reflect the views or perspective of those who are mentioned in the book.

Beauty From Ashes Media

Burleson, TX 76028

Paperback Edition 2020

ISBN: 9798655933736

Copyright © Andi Cook, 2020

Editing and Proofreading by Andria Flores

Cover Design by Lexi Cepak

Up From the Ashes

by

ANDI COOK

Beauty From Ashes Media

<h1 style="text-align:center">ACKNOWLEDGEMENTS</h1>

I would like to extend my deepest appreciation to a few special people in my life that made this journey possible:

Country, you are my heart and my whole world. I love you with all that I am. We have faced the world together, fighting through everything life threw at us. We have suffered together and celebrated together... but no matter what, we stuck together and God brought us through victoriously every time. I am so very proud of the young man you have become. You are an amazing human, a truly awesome man of God. The future is bright son; you **will** accomplish great things.

To my parents, you are my rock – thank you both for your unwavering love and encouragement. Thank you for supporting me every step of the way. You never let me give up, even when I wanted to. You never let me embrace complacency and always coached, mentored, and pushed me forward to discover what God had planned for my life. Words cannot express how much you mean to me. I love you both so very much.

To my first mentors in life: Rob Johnston, Holly Johnston, Jim Clayton, Lincoln Clayton, and Jeanie Gilbert French. Without each of you, I would never have made it through the confusion of adolescents or the darkness of depression that I fought as a teen in a very difficult situation. Each of you taught me about love, courage, and strength. To each of you, I am who I am today because of you.

To my siblings: Elicia, Mathew, and Kim, you have taken this journey with me every step of the way and have each given me strength and courage during different times in my life. **Elicia,** it's been me and you since we shared a room as kids. The only person I have ever met with as much of a generous heart and "we can fix this together" attitude is Grandad. He was so proud of you. I am proud of you for your career accomplishments, for your own journey to healing, and for your passion and compassion. **Mathew,** if you would have told me that you'd be the one that ended up with six kids and a crazy busy life of ministry and parenthood, I wouldn't have believed you. Turns out, you're really good at all of it. I am proud of the husband and father that you are, and I am absolutely thrilled to see you living out God's calling on your life. As you continue to walk out God's plan for your life, you are changing the world around you, and I stand with you in celebration and can't wait to see what God does next. **Kim,** my sister from another mister, I will never forget the day that your dad married my mom, because I got the coolest sister friend in the whole wide world. I don't know what I'd do without you and our crazy text, meme exchanges and 30 second pep talks. When life happens, good or bad, it's you I reach out to first. Our hearts are always *and have always been* connected. I admire your strength and courage. I love you, and I am so proud of you.

To my editor Andria Flores, it is hard to believe that in a few short months, you took the roughest rough draft ever and coached it into a book. Not only is the book better because of you, but *I* am better because of you. You pushed me beyond my comfort zone and challenged me to dig deeper emotionally. You are a blessing to my life. Thank you for being my editor. Thank you for being a dear friend.

DEDICATION

This book is dedicated to Lisa Pilgrim – my sixth-grade English teacher. Thank you for helping me find to my writing voice and words of power when I needed them most. Though you may not feel worthy of this accomplishment, it is only a very small token of my appreciation for your hard work and dedication to the students of Burleson ISD for thirty years.

Table of Contents

I started writing this book as a simple journal to document my own journey to mental and emotional health. It began as a private journal; I never intended to share it with the world, and I *certainly* never intended to share it with the Church. *Up From the Ashes* contains intimate details of my life, including how God redeemed and ultimately transformed my thought patterns, habits, choices, and lifestyle. I no longer hide from the people I perceive to be unhappy with me and somewhere in the healing process, I quit running when circumstances seem tougher than what I believed I can handle. Someone once told me, "You've always been tenacious; you just don't like to get dirty." Ouch. Granted, they were being completely honest, their comment stung. As a self-proclaimed overcomer, I felt like I could rally through even the biggest challenges; however, when I took a long hard look at my past choices, I realized that I had my Nikes on standby at all times. I was *actually* an emotional runner. I was a strong runner. I was even a runner with purpose. But when the going got tough, really tough, I got out.

I shied away from tough conversations because I was afraid of losing relationships. However, through healing and gaining the confidence that came from rooting my identity in Christ, I have learned to have difficult conversations that include hard truths and what I call "fearless feedback". It's the kind of feedback I give when I care so much about a person that I am willing to fight, yell, make them mad, and even slam a few doors to confront issues that need to be dealt with. With all my heart, I believe that the issues that I write about in this book desperately need to be talked about especially among Christians. The Church is filled with hurting souls who are searching for answers and someone to start a dialogue that says, "You don't have to walk this path alone. I have been where you are."

Once I knew God was leading me to share my story publicly, it took months before I gained the courage to speak in full transparency about my weaknesses, insecurities, struggles, failures, and mistakes. I was terrified to speak openly about the most painful parts of my history. I wasn't ready to talk about any of it really, but God had other plans, so talk about it, we shall. I struggled—make that a full caps STRUGGLED—with what I would say in this book. I was emotionally paralyzed with the fear that I would face harsh judgment and criticism from those within the Church whose lives were a lot more put together than my own, and whose closets had a few less skeletons.

When God first put it on my heart to go bold with full scriptural references and transparent details, I full on Jonah-revolted. I had recently read a horrible Buzz Feed article on one of my "sheroes," Rachel Hollis. The writer crucified Rachel for her journey and her message, and the comments from the public were even worse. That only solidified my fear that the Church would tear me apart and that those outside of the Church would be cruel. I have a lot of friends in the Church, and I have a lot of friends who want nothing to do with the Church. I didn't want to be caught in an "us vs. them" war between the Church and those who may have been wounded by it.

However, last year I accepted that my faith is part of my journey, a really important part, and could not be left out of this message. I didn't grow up in a church culture that embraced talking about deep rooted emotional battles. My life is a living example of why we need better support systems and an open dialogue among God's people. God began to show me that His people are hurting in silence all over the world. They need a message of hope and a testimony of redemption. I believe God is looking on the Church and that He isn't entirely thrilled about everything He sees in us. If you don't believe me, spend five minutes on Twitter looking at Beth Moore's feed and see the things Christians and other ministers say to and about her. #ChristiansAreMean. If Twitter were my only introduction into what Christianity was all about, I probably wouldn't want to be a Christian. However, I am on a mission to partner with God's people to change that. I want to ignite a movement that sparks healing and spreads the love of Jesus.

I believe that one of the most ironic truths about the Church is that while denominations are imploding over marriage rights and women in leadership, mainstream media and artists are embracing love, peace, and harmony in the greatest kumbaya-movement since Michael Jackson and Lionel Richie partnered with 45 celebrities to record "We Are the World" in 1985. That song brought the entire world together and went quadruple platinum, all while raising more than $63 million dollars for the War Against World Famine. It worked because unity works.

While it's true that we live in a country that is so divided it's hard to find a middle ground, we cannot perpetuate dissention. When non-believers are waving the "love and accept everyone" flag, we as the Church should be the first in line to say, "Hey, we're in! That's our thing!" The answer to conflict must lie with us as Christians to reach out in love, kindness, and compassion so we can embrace people and show them the unfailing, never ending, precious love of God that we sing about on Sundays. We were called to do two things on this earth: love God and love people. It's really that simple.

Some of my story may shock you, and that's okay because some of it shocked me when it happened. We are still going to power through and talk about it. You may become angry with me about some of the choices I made—and boy, there have been some doozies. I understand that. I have done some pretty terrible things in my life, but I can't hide that. Only telling you part of the story won't really do justice to demonstrate how much God has done in my life, what He brought me through, or the full power of His redeeming grace. I am going to be transparent and brutally honest about tragedies that have happened to me and the choices I made that led me to a place of brokenness and desperation. I am going to talk about it, because we need to start talking about real stuff that people in the congregation and sitting in the seats beside us are carrying with them.

I am going to fearlessly answer the calling God has on my life because I know that somewhere right now is a young lady making a plan to end her life because the secrets she carries are too much of a burden for her to bear. I cringe to think that she may have reached out for help, hope, and answers, but that she may not have found them, even within the walls of the Church. She may be so bound up with fear of judgement, guilt, and shame, just like I was, that she can't bring herself to take down the walls around her heart.

In all that I have ever survived, I had one prayer: "God use this to help someone else with what they are facing. Take these ashes of my life and make something beautiful. Use me and all of this pain." He has. Every time my story helps someone else with what they are facing, God is keeping His promise to me that He would turn my pain into something beautiful. This is the story of how God brought me Up From the Ashes.

I Think I'm Broken

On July 4, 2017, I sat on the tailgate of my son's truck in a small parking lot in Burleson, Texas. It was just the three of us, my son, my sister, and myself, as so many adventures had been through the years. We enjoyed the sunset and listened to country music on the radio while we waited for the fireworks to begin. I watched families laughing together. Children ran happily with sparklers glittering through the air as they weaved through the small crowds of parents and siblings. The sweet sound of giggles and squeals of delight blended with the music perfectly. My son, seventeen at the time, was proud that he was able to drive us to the show in his own truck. He stayed closed to the cab to control the radio while he sang and danced in his usual silly way. He made being seventeen look careless and free. Next to me was my sister, who shared my fondness for July 4th. The weather was perfect. Everything seemed perfect. In all of the nostalgia and excitement, I should have felt happy. At the very minimum I should have felt content, at least that's what I told myself sitting on the tailgate feeling only one thing: empty.

My sister, who knows me better than almost anyone, knew something wasn't right. She didn't ask what was wrong. That's not really her way. She simply asked, "How can I help?" It was an understood acknowledgement that she saw me; she saw that I was hurting. I wasn't pressured to open up or dive deep into conversation, it was just a simple, graceful question of where I needed her most in whatever I was facing. The journey that I have taken toward overcoming anxiety and depression started that day as I faintly whispered, "I think I'm broken," without even looking her direction.

Elicia has had courtside seats to every event in my life. She, more than anyone, knew and understood my brokenness. However, she never let me forget that I am not entirely broken. I am a strong woman who has endured a life of tragedy and heartache but learned how to succeed anyway. God used the stories of my past to weave together a beautiful tapestry in my heart. He drew threads from childhood abuse, and from thirty years of reliving it in my sleep almost every night and wove them together with the remnants of having my heart broken more times than I care to admit. These threads are sewn together and intertwined with threads of a failed marriage and even a separate abusive marriage. *Yep...two marriages, two failures, lots of threads.* Then He pulled the tattered threads from five miscarriages, including one at 20 weeks, and continued to create a beautiful tapestry from my tragedy. He fulfilled His promise to create beauty from the ashes of my life.

God guided my steps as I dug my way out of poverty, and He opened doors for me to create a fulfilling career that I love. There are remnants that represent my victory over an intense self-harm addiction. Only He saw the tears I cried as I battled my weight for more than two decades and lost over a hundred pounds twice, once in less than six months. Only, I can't celebrate it because I gained it ALL back. The tapestry continues with threads that remain from medication-dependent anxiety, diagnosed PTSD, a teenage eating disorder, and a life-long battle with depression. God continued to create an intricate masterpiece in the form of a testimony when He carried me through a ninety-six-day migraine which paralyzed my whole left side and marked the beginning of a ten-year battle with a super-rare debilitating migraine disorder.

The end result, the testimony and ministry that stemmed from trauma and tragedy that God carried me through. I am living in victory every day because I didn't give up half-way through the battle when life became unbearable. I had to lean into the discomfort, knowing that growth happens outside of my comfort zone.

The most serious struggle I can personally address is the paralyzing battles with depression, anxiety, mental illness, and loss of hope. In my own fight, I had to get and accept the help I needed. I made informed decisions with the help of medical professionals, my pastoral team, counselors, and coaches. I learned the importance of seeking medical advice from a well-informed medical team. I was empowered by honesty as I acknowledged that I didn't have to face my battles alone, that I *should* not face my battles alone. I had a tribe who surrounded me in love and carried me when I was too weak to continue fighting on my own.

My journey led me to become a Certified Life Coach to help others identify and remove the roadblocks that prevent them from reaching their goals. When I speak with a client for the first time, I begin our coaching session with these words, "Your story belongs to you, and I won't presume to know its impact on your life. I can tell you that if you've found yourself at rock bottom looking for answers, I have been there. I never saw a path leading out, so I had to create an exit route by making a path back up life's mountain. The trail was blazed with a lot of hard lessons and even more heartaches. I would be honored to partner with you in your journey and show you the path I took to find healing and freedom."

I have a long history of taking on projects that I am not fully prepared for, like when I accepted my first management role and had absolutely no idea the magnitude of what I was getting myself into. There were many times I wanted to quit that job, but I knew I was there for a reason. My mom has often said that we are in situations to either learn something or teach something, and we have to figure out which one it is. I was there to learn. My perfectionist nature caused me to get defensive as an ill-equipped corporate leader when I felt inadequate or perceived that someone was telling me I did something wrong. I didn't give myself the grace of a learning curve, instead I forged ahead with a no-excuses attitude.

I had an employee who was difficult to manage. Multiple managers with an impressive amount of experience and credentials had attempted to work with him; they all failed miserably. I actually liked him as an employee because he was serious about his work, but he was definitely a challenge for my first leadership role. Heading into HR to address a formal complaint filed against him was a common occurrence because he was, well, abrasive in his approach. When he had a goal to accomplish, he didn't let anyone, or their feelings, get in his way.

Before one particular meeting that I was dreading, I sat at my desk feeling super-nervous while trying to prepare my mind to receive advice from the HR manager about dealing with the situation. I was defensive because I felt like I was supposed to be able to handle the problem on my own. I shut down good advice sometimes because I felt inadequate. While admittedly the HR manager's approach was not always the best, there was truly good advice in her message. As I prayed before that meeting and asked God to soften my heart and help me not put up walls of defense, I felt God give me peace. I scrolled out the letters "B-O-N-D" across the top of the notepad that I would take with me into the meeting. BOND—Be Open, Not Defensive—became one of my life mottos.

I walked into the meeting prepared to receive fearless feedback and harsh truths. The message was every bit as abrasive as I had prepared for, but every time I looked down at my notepad, I saw the letters BOND and fought the defensiveness that tried to creep into my heart and mind. I fought to listen past the words she spoke so I could hear the message she intended. I could have gotten mad and stormed out. I would have been justified in that, but I would have missed an important lesson that I honestly needed to hear.

Through that experience, I learned to incorporate BOND into my life and thought patterns. When I feel myself getting defensive, I try to remind myself to take a deep breath and remain open-minded instead of allowing myself to get defensive. While writing this book, I noticed BONDing opportunities where my story or message might be hard for others to hear. When I answered the calling God placed on my life, I made several promises to myself and to Him. First, I promised that I would not write about anything that I had not personally walked through. My second commitment was to tell my whole story, not just the easy parts. Third, I promised to only write my own story. It may seem obvious, but I can only tell my story from my perspective.

I tend to intuit what I perceive others are feeling or thinking in response to me. However, that's my truth, not necessarily theirs. For example, I might go out in public with a messy bun and no makeup on and feel like someone is totally judging me and posting my picture on the People of Walmart page. In truth, most people don't care that it looks like I have never owned a hairbrush in my life because their life doesn't revolve around me. However, my own insecurity may be shining through and causing me to feel like the whole world has an opinion about my fashion choices, or lack thereof.

Keeping those promises to myself required open, honest, and vulnerable soul searching. I had to embrace BONDing completely. I didn't want to justify my actions or explain away mistakes. My goal was to shine a light on how God brought me through the challenges that I didn't think I was strong enough to even face, much less conquer. I wanted to share a powerful story of how I overcame being trapped inside my own mind, held captive by overthinking perfectionist thoughts. For up from the ashes I rose...and soared.

One of my favorite symbols is the phoenix, which literally means *out of the ashes*. I use that symbol for my radio show, my life group, and my blog. I even named my red Camaro *Phoenix* when I bought it in 2016. The phoenix is a symbol of the promise God gave us all to create beauty from the ashes in our lives. When my life was all messed up and without hope, I knew there had to be actions I could take to get out of the place I had been, so I could go where I was called to be.

CHAPTER TWO

The Faintest Ink

Mary Kay Ash is one of my *sheroes* because she literally made an empire, or *fempire* if you will, out of nothing. In 1963 she had grown weary of training men who would promote above her in a workplace that did not celebrate the talents or successes of women. She made a $5,000 investment, hired nine salespeople, and opened a small store in Dallas, Texas with her son. Over time, that investment turned into a company that has more than 1.5 million representatives and revenue exceeding $3.5 billion. When I see someone like Mary Kay Ash, who found the courage, talent, and fortitude to bring their biggest, most unattainable dreams to fruition, I take note of how they accomplished it. The first lesson I learned from Mary Kay was to "find something you love so much you would do it for free, and someone will pay you well for it." That concept has driven my career decisions for two decades. The second piece of advice was that the faintest ink is better than the most retentive memory, or in other words, write stuff down.

When I sat out to transform my life, I needed a way to organize the thoughts that cycled through my mind. Journaling was the most logical and comfortable place for me to start documenting my course. Daily entries provided an overview of my habits and thoughts. I was able to identify problem areas and decide what actions I wanted to take to change my trajectory. I learned quickly that if I was going to remove a negative habit from my life, I had to replace it with something positive. For example, when I gave up processed carbs (which is something I used to do unsuccessfully a few times a year), I had to replace the carbs with something healthier in order to finally kick the habit. So, I learned to replace tortilla chips with cherry tomatoes, so I still had something to dip in guacamole and didn't have to completely give up one of my favorite foods. *I mean, sometimes a girl just needs guac in her life.*

Or what about when I got the bright idea to stop cursing? Y'all, let's have our first BOND moment here. *Be open, not defensive.* I don't think God falls off His throne because we spout out a four-letter word. I don't think the Holy Spirit leaves us when we rant and rave and cry out in anger and frustration to God. After all, God designed us to come to Him when we're in distress. I'm not just saying that because I had a serious struggle to control my mouth, or that the phrase "I love Jesus, but I cuss a little" totally applied to me. To keep it real, my selective use of profanity bordered on absolute hilarity, and at times, I kind of miss it. However, I didn't want my language to be a distraction from my message, and I was slightly terrified that I'd cuss in a pulpit somewhere while speaking publicly.

So while I have absolutely no judgement about people using profanity, because my faith is not so fragile that I'm derailed by an F-bomb, I thought I might give the critics one less thing to blast me about in the comments section of my sound clips, or to confront me about in the foyer after church. *Sorry, not sorry.* Back to replacing bad behaviors with good ones, I set out on a mission to control my mouth and got pretty darn creative with adjectives. In truth, it wasn't as hard as I thought it would be, unless I was stuck in traffic, stubbed my toe in the middle of the night, or the time I ripped an acrylic fingernail completely off, taking my natural nail with it, and I invented brand new combinations of curse words.

To kick my four-letter word habit, I had to find a way to express myself, and after dropping some of my most colorful adjectives, I needed a healthy way to get my feelings out. So, I journaled. For the longest time, my diary was the only place I felt I could be real. I could yell, cuss, and scream, and nobody would have an opinion about it. It was truly the first step I took in getting healthy. I committed to myself that I would take time every day for therapeutic writing and reflection. Journaling helped me with the creative problem-solving process by enabling me to organize my thoughts and sort out my feelings in a safe way. Additionally, it provided historic references for reflection and celebrating progress. I have also seen success with journaling in multiple formats from my coaching clients who have documented their progress using creative journaling formats like vlogging, blogging, drawing, or creating music.

Through my journal, I identified patterns of behavior that detracted from my goals. I wanted to change those habits by replacing them with healthier ones. When I identified great habits, I used them as building blocks to develop healthy routines. Through daily reflection, a solid action plan, recreating my habits, and adding in daily affirmations, I began to take ownership of my life. I removed the excuses that enabled me to procrastinate or quit. One of my trainers at Camp Gladiator used to say that if you want something bad enough, you will find a reason, but if you don't, you'll find an excuse. I became goal-focused, and my reasons to succeed pushed me harder than my excuses to quit.

I listened to Rachel Hollis' recording of her book *Girl, Wash Your Face*, and while she doesn't know it yet, she's absolutely one of my mentors because she helped me see something that I was incredibly guilty of. Rachel described being a person who broke promises to herself so often that her subconscious didn't separate intentions from ideas. I jumped through a million hoops to keep commitments that I made to others, but I found a million excuses why I could put off the promises I made to myself. Somehow completing a report for my boss was worth going through hell to accomplish, but when it came to personal tasks like writing this book, going on diets, meal prepping, starting exercise plans, setting better boundaries, forming better routines, or breaking bad habits, I couldn't muster the energy or the courage to start. Looking back, I can laugh about the fact that I literally procrastinated the decision to stop procrastinating.

I have always been an all-in kind of girl. I'm either jumping in with both feet or I'm all out. There is no middle ground for me. I'm that crazy person who is like, *I think I'll start running. Let's train for a marathon!* To be totally fair to myself, it wasn't an actual marathon that I trained for, it was more like a 5k who wanted to be a marathon when it grew up. For obvious reasons, that was a terrible idea and completely fell flat because I didn't go through the steps required before going all in. Going from no activity at all to running a 5k is not a natural progression. I didn't have a foundation to build on. As with most things in my life, I tried to build a house from the roof down.

I have made a lot of really great decisions at really terrible times, which led to overcommitment and burn out because I took on too many responsibilities with far too

23

few resources. For someone who had absolutely zero belief in herself, I was really quick to take on seemingly impossible tasks that I was totally ill-equipped to handle, but somehow thought I could. In her book, Rachel Hollis talked about that too. She said that the solution started with finding something small to commit to for a set period of time, and then just do it—keep that commitment. She said it would help to rebuild the trust in myself that I had damaged over the years by lack of follow through. Journaling became my small commitment.

I chose journaling because I knew it would work as a replacement behavior when I was stressed out. It substituted for some of my other bad habits, like heading to the fridge to stress eat. It also helped me process my feelings when I was tempted to self-harm. I selected journaling because there were very few excuses that I could dream up that would prevent me from getting it done. There would never be a night when I was like, "I really wanted to journal today, but it's raining, so I just can't." The "no pen, no paper" excuse was eliminated by planning in advance. I had pens in my purse. I wrote on napkins at restaurants. I grabbed blank paper at my parents' house to write on. I even resorted to writing on the back of envelopes while sitting in my car in my own driveway because I knew once I went in the house, life would explode, and I honestly wouldn't get to it. My journal entries weren't complicated. My first Empowerment Journal looked like this:

My empowered life began on February 27th, 2017
Three things I am currently struggling with that I will find a solution for:
1) I am miserable at work

2) I am having daily panic attacks

3) I am self-harming 4-5 times per day

Three things that have happened in my past that I will turn into my testimony:

1) Childhood Abuse

2) Two Failed Marriages

3) Five Miscarriages, including losing Caden

Three things that I have done well or that I have had a breakthrough in:

1) Overcoming Hemiplegic Migraines

2) Getting out of poverty level income

3) Learning how to become the best parent for Alex

Three traits that I am improving:

1) Impatience

2) Fear

3) Insecurity

On this journey, I want to learn: how to change my thought processes where I am not struggling every day with fear and anxiety. I want to be able to stop taking medication to control how I feel, and I want to be in control of my mind and my thoughts. I want to find my purpose and passion in life again and wake up every day ready to face the world and fulfill my destiny in life.

I am willing to invest: at least one hour every day to listening to positive messages and documenting my journey. I am willing to humble myself, accept help, and learn. I am willing to change my habits with the way I manage my finances and my time. I am willing to risk having to change every single thing about myself in order to become exactly who I am called to be.

For me, motivation is directly tied to my progress, which is why I thrive in metrics driven environments.

When the goals are clear and the action plan is reasonable, I am almost unstoppable. Knowing that about myself, I made sure that I included an honest reflection, a goal, a plan, and a commitment in each entry. I made sure to celebrate success because that helped me maintain focus on the big picture. I was honest with myself about what I was struggling with for the first time in my whole life, which was much harder than I thought it would be.

I was the queen of compartmentalizing, so to face the pain that I had spent most of my life running from meant that I had to overcome my natural flight instinct. It also meant that I had to build trust with myself beyond just believing that I would keep my promises. I had to establish that my mind was a safe space for my own thoughts and exploration. I had to create trust that if I allowed myself to think and feel freely, I was safe from judgment within my own mind, and that if I allowed raw vulnerable honesty, I would not self-destruct.

BOND with me here, I am pretty sure I am not the only one in the world who feels like they are their own worst enemy. If I sat down with my best friend and revealed my deepest struggles to her, and she responded as cruelly as the way I talked to myself, it would destroy our friendship. I was a great friend to others, but it turns out, I was the worst friend I have ever had. I was in an emotionally abusive relationship with myself. I had to learn to extend the same grace and mercy to myself that I would to any of my friends. I had to learn to become my own best friend and my own biggest cheerleader—not in an "I don't need anyone" kind of way, but in an "I'm not going to be the person who says the worst things about me" kind of way.

Journaling helped me identify the negative thoughts that perpetuated the negative image I had of myself.

Writing was the first coping strategy I ever learned. Writing for healing began for me when I was in the sixth grade and saw a Christian Counselor for the first time. Life as my family knew it had changed overnight. At twelve years old, I faced adult decisions and situations that children should never have to experience, like testifying to a District Attorney and Sherriff about deeply personal things that I knew could get someone I loved in a lot of trouble. I faced harsh realities looking through the tainted lens of a child's perception that led to guilt. The message that I embraced at the time was that I had ruined everything. I had told my father's secrets, and everything changed because of me.

CHAPTER THREE

Cracked Foundations

During my final year of elementary school, I wasn't a carefree girl experimenting with makeup and gossiping happily on the playground with my classmates. I was struggling with deep, troubling feelings of guilt, anger, and fear about the future of my entire family. For three years I had endured sexual abuse at the hands of my biological father. In his full-time career, he was a truck driver who sometimes took me on the road with him, but what impacted me most was that he was also a Children's Pastor at our church. His actions broke my entire foundation for love, trust, faith, God, sex, fatherhood, family, and forgiveness. I know at times I can be hyperbolic, but I am being literal when I say that everything in my heart that had been pure and innocent before he abused me was shattered into hundreds of unrecognizable pieces.

At just twelve years old, I felt completely out of control in my life. While the abuse had actually stopped before I reported it, the impact it had on me remained. Fear of what I would dream about kept me awake at night, and once I finally drifted off to sleep, nightmares would wake me up panting, sweating, and crying. There were other effects too. I avoided being alone with men. My biological father's volatile temper terrified me. Fear held me captive in silence as the secret bearer. Depression forced out any hope I had of my family returning to a rhythm that made sense to my young mind.

To completely understand what happened, we have to start when I was seven with how my entire concept of sex became incredibly distorted. My first introduction to sex happened while watching an episode of *Little House on the Prairie* where one of Albert's friends was sexually assaulted. The questions I asked my parents about what I had seen on TV led them to sit down and have "the talk" with my brother, sister, and me. Our talk was complete with scientific words and pictures from the encyclopedia. A traumatizing conversation that stemmed from me seeing a PG version of sexual assault, combined with the mechanics of sex, created the perception in my seven-year-old mind that sex was not mutually enjoyable for both people. I concluded that it was a horrible thing that happened when a boy made a girl do something she didn't want to—and she cried.

Fast forward two years later to when my biological father first violated my trust. Up to that point, I was a straight A student who stayed out of the way to steer clear of his explosive temper. The first time I remember him being inappropriate was one day when I stayed home sick from school. He offered me five dollars to undress in front of him. I did not...and it was the first time in my young life that I didn't do what one my parents asked me to. I can remember how uncomfortable it made me feel, but at nine years old, I didn't understand the implications of what he had asked for. I knew instinctively that I wasn't supposed to talk about it, and I didn't tell anyone what happened that day. In fact, I ran into the other room and didn't come out until my mom got home, and then I pretended like nothing had happened at all.

I equated disappearing to safety. When I was yelled at, I stared at the floor in silence. When others were fighting, I stayed away. I didn't catch as much of the brunt of my biological father's rage as my brother and sister did because I made sure I was as far out of sight as possible. I remember experiencing my fair share of extreme punishments, like spankings with weight belts that left large welts and bruises; being slapped across my face for screaming at my brother; or being spanked with objects that were not meant for spanking, like 2X4 boards, cords, hangers, and cutting boards. However, I don't remember the degree of physical punishments happening to me like they did for my siblings. While disappearing worked for me that day, it wouldn't work later when his behavior advanced to much more inappropriate and violent acts.

After his behavior escalated, I didn't know where to go for help. Still nine years old, I sat on the school playground with one of my best friends, and I told her that my father was "raping" me. The fact was that his behavior had only consisted of very inappropriate touching and sexual acts. Penetration is an important distinction with prosecuting attorneys, but not as clear in the heart of a little girl who had once seen her dad as her hero. His actions had not crossed the line to rape, but at nine, I didn't know the difference. All I knew was that what was happening to me matched the concept that had formed in my mind when I saw that episode of *Little House on the Prairie*.

My friend told our school counselor, and soon I was called in and questioned. The school leadership called my brother and sister in as well and asked them about our home life. It was somewhere around 1988 or 1989 before many laws and regulations were put in place to protect children, and certainly before those laws were carried out in small towns. Because my mom was an active member of the PTO, the school counselor and principal decided to call her and share my accusations with her instead of reporting them. That night was awful.

My biological father denied the accusations and became irate. My mom was furious and didn't know what to believe. The focus was on the word *rape*, which was explained to me in great detail, and I was quick to say, "No, that is not what happened." However, I did not offer any further details about what actually took place. Out of fear, I recanted my whole story. I simply said I was lying about the whole thing. I accepted the consequences of lying and disappeared to the safety of my shell again. Later when we were alone, he asked me, "Did you honestly think that's what rape was? I'll show you what it is." He later made good on that threat.

If anyone were standing outside our living room window looking in, they would have seen how well we all interacted with one another, including my biological father and me. From the outside, it appeared everything was fine. He was my dad. I loved him. That's what made the abuse so earth shattering—because we had a close relationship. To protect my family, I learned to pretend. I learned to keep my mouth shut, and I adopted my biological father's motto, "What happens in the family, stays in the family." Those words make my stomach turn, even now.

The abuse continued for two more years. I felt like I was the only one dealing with the aftermath. He didn't seem phased. Life went on as if nothing had happened. I thought that my biological father got to just live a normal life while I was a mess. One day in sixth grade, I finally told my friend Lisa about the abuse, and how I had become terrified that it would happen again. Lisa was brave, and though I made her swear to never tell anyone, she was smart and knew that she couldn't keep *that* secret to herself. She told our D.A.R.E. officer at school, and the next thing I knew my family life was upside down again. My biological father was removed from our home, and my mom was given a long list of rules to follow and threats that if she didn't do everything CPS wanted, they would take custody of us.

CPS mandated that I attend individual counseling and participate in a support group for young victims of sexual violence. I did not have a good therapeutic experience. It took me years to reprogram my thinking that "just because I was abused meant that I would marry an abuser." Despite the staggering statistics, it didn't have to be that way; there was another option. They said it over and over and over though, "You were abused. You're going to marry an abuser." I hated going to therapy, and I vowed that if I were destined to marry an abuser, I just wouldn't get married.

While on some level it was good to be in a room with other young ladies who had been through similar traumatic experiences, I didn't feel more equipped to deal with problems as a result of going. However, there was one counselor who I saw only twice, yet she made a significant impact on my life. She quickly identified that I had a hard time expressing my true thoughts and feelings. *If you know me now, you know that I have **fully** recovered from that!* The therapist knew that if I was going to survive with minimal life scars, I had to find a way to identify how I felt and to express all that was bottled up inside of me. She suggested that I start journaling and asked me to write letters to the people who had hurt me. I came back the next week and read them to her.

She smiled kindly and congratulated my effort, but she didn't let it slide that I only talked about the facts, and not the feelings. I remember her gentle tone of voice when she said, "No, you need to talk about how you *feel,* not just the mechanics or facts of what took place. Don't say what you think you're supposed to say, say what you *need* to say. Write everything that you wish you could say to your dad." Through my writing, I found ways to express pain, sadness, anger, and fear. I also learned how to express when I was proud of myself or wanted to celebrate a victory. I learned to experience emotions without being controlled by them. Today, as I type the story that I thought I would never be strong enough to tell publicly, I know I would not have made it this far without the counselor who challenged me to express myself and the English teacher who taught me how to do just that.

CHAPTER FOUR

Plot Twists

Life's plot twists became the chapters of my story, which then created the book of my life. I began to cope with my emotions by writing fictional novels of characters who had overcome what I was going through. My sixth grade English teacher, Lisa Pilgrim, took my handwritten manuscripts and edited them for me. She offered feedback and pushed me to explore the story lines. She was a ray of hope in a very dark year of my life. By facing my own challenges through the characters in the stories I wrote, I was able to face the real events that I didn't know how to process. Through fiction, a great counselor, and the kindness of an educator going above and beyond, I was starting to heal. In fact, the reason I dedicate this book to Lisa Pilgrim is for her years of service to Burleson ISD, and for that 1991-1992 school year that I don't think I would have made it through without her.

Unfortunately, the plot twists for our family weren't over. After my biological father was arrested and released from jail, he sat down with the pastors of our church. Together, they made the decision that God forgives even the vilest sin, and they allowed him to continue his leadership role as Children's Pastor for the next year under the condition that he continued counseling and attended the court-ordered group therapy sessions. The Bible makes it clear that what is done in the dark will come to light. It did, and it did not turn out well.

I struggled to find hope. I honestly didn't feel I had a reason to live. My Youth Group quickly became my support system. I promoted to Youth the summer before seventh grade. Soon after, our church hired a new Youth Pastor. I attended every Youth function they offered, but as each event would wind down and the time would come to go home, I became withdrawn and depressed. My biological father had fulfilled all of the CPS requirements in order to move back home. Our house was filled with fighting again. I quickly lost hope.

The first night I met Rob Johnston, our Youth Pastor, I was sitting in the hallway just outside the door that led to the fellowship hall in our church. The rest of the members of our youth group were inside having Prayer and Pizza. I was close enough to hear their laughter, but far enough away to remain unnoticed. It sounded like they were having the time of their lives, and I questioned why I couldn't experience carefree joy in the way they did. I didn't feel how it sounded like they felt. I sat with my head tilted back against the wall, wondering how many more times I could go home. I didn't know how much longer I could go through the motions of trying to put everything back together, when I really wanted to be as far away from my biological father as possible. In the solitude of the hallway of our church that Sunday night, I planned how I would end my life.

When Rob walked down the hallway past me, he stopped quickly, took me by the hand, and pulled me to my feet. I remember the kind smile on his face when he opened the door to an empty Sunday School room and said, "Step into my office." I couldn't tell you what he said to me that day, or how he knew how close I was to ending my life, but I remember feeling a glimmer of hope in our simple conversation. When I left, I felt connected and safe for the first time in a very long time. Rob exuded Christ-like love and had a broad, joyous smile. When he introduced me to his wife Holly that night, I thought she was the sweetest, most beautiful woman I had ever seen. She radiated kindness and love. She was absolutely regal, and she was my instant hero, and immediately I had the beginnings of a new extended family. More importantly, I had hope.

As time progressed, several church members found out about the abuse and decided to leave the church. Naturally, they did not want their children learning about faith from a sex offender. Rightfully so. As a parent looking back on the whole situation, I can't imagine the scene of outrage that I would have caused upon finding out about the close contact my child had with a sex offender—at church, no less. The first family to leave the church did so quietly. Even though their anger was justified, and they had every right to make a scene, they chose to leave discreetly to avoid bringing further shame on my siblings and me.

The church leaders had no choice but to remove my biological father from leadership or face losing their congregation in the fallout. Our Senior Pastor was on sabbatical during all of this, but there was no way to prolong the decision until his return. They asked for my biological father's resignation. He was devasted. Ministers, doctors, counselors, family, and friends had all told my parents that God could redeem my biological father and restore our family. They all encouraged the goal of full restoration and healing. It was the unified plan we were all moving toward. We all played our parts and did exactly what was expected of us to put the pieces back together.

The night after the church asked for his resignation, something changed in him, and he gave up all hope for restoration. There was a huge fight at our house that night. I don't remember most of the harsh words that were yelled or who yelled them. I do remember the angry words I said that night. The message I internalized in my heart and mind was that this was all my fault, even though nobody said that out loud.

Confronted with his own shame over what he had done, the public knowledge that he was a sex offender, the loss of his sense of purpose, and the shattering of his hope, he got on his motorcycle and just rode. I think he rode without a destination in mind, that he just kept riding until he couldn't ride any longer. My biological father ended up in a motel in Nebraska, where he wrote his final goodbye in a note to my mom before he committed suicide.

He had disappeared on May 4th, died on May 5th, and on May 6th, two police officers came to our house to make the notification. Those forty-eight hours of waiting and not knowing how to feel were torture. To know he was gone, suspect that he planned to end his life, but not have a way to reach him, was utter torment. This was long before the time of cell phones. There wasn't a way to track him or know where he was, but I think we all knew that he was gone. In fact, as the officers came inside our home, I looked at them blankly and asked, "He's dead, isn't he?" I didn't cry. I couldn't cry. At just thirteen years of age, I fully carried the weight of killing my father. I blamed myself for telling, for fighting—and even worse, for feeling relieved that I was safer because he was gone. I didn't have to be afraid anymore. It took more than ten years before I stopped blaming myself for his death.

In the days following his death, I went into hostess mode as people visited our house. I took care of everyone else. I made plates of food and served drinks, ensuring everyone was as comfortable as possible. I tried to ease their grief and fix the pain that I felt I caused. I only remember sitting still one time after our home filled with family and church friends. Out of all the people who came and went those days, I most remember the Associate Pastor's wife. She sat close to me on the couch with a supportive arm around me and didn't say a single word to me. She talked to others, but not to me. She just offered graceful, silent strength that I remember so vividly. Janet exuded peace. I felt safe. I didn't have to answer questions or explain anything. She redirected people who tried to hover over me. She was exactly what I needed at that time.

At night after the guests would leave and the house would get strangely quiet, I would go to my room alone, and journal to process the feelings that warred inside of me. Guilt ate away at me daily. Guilt turned into resentment, which eventually turned into apathy. I learned to walk around with a smile on my face. I learned to be silly so nobody would ask that dreaded "How are you?" question with their infuriating looks of sympathy. The only time I let my feelings show was when I would write. Again, I found myself relying on fictional characters in the stories I wrote. It would take another twenty-five years, and a whole lot of heartache, before I would find the voice to say out loud that it had indeed all happened, and that it actually happened to me.

CHAPTER FIVE

Bonus Family

It took years for my family to work through the wounds and scars left behind in the aftermath of abuse and my biological father's suicide. I had to work through my own feelings about my family. We had to create a new normal and heal together before we could move forward. Today, my mom is absolutely one of my heroes. She is an incredible woman, but it took time and maturity for me to accept that. As a young adult, I had to reconcile my unresolved emotions regarding my mom. I blamed her during most of my teen years for not stopping the abuse. I was mad at her because I felt like she hadn't believed me when I was nine.

Looking back from an adult's perspective, I don't think for one minute that she knew about the abuse until it was too late. The only indication that there was a problem was the first time I told, but I had fully recanted my story and worked overtime to convince everyone that it had all been a lie. And of course, my biological father did his part to convince her of his complete innocence. I think my brother explained it best when he told me, "It's one thing to know that you were married to someone with a bad temper, maybe even to admit that you married a jerk, but it's an entirely different story to look at the person that you vowed to spend the rest of your life with, and realize that you married a monster."

My mom just accepted my anger, she apologized time and time again. She didn't defend or justify. She stuck to the facts that she had not known about the abuse and that she would have made sure it stopped if she had known.

Several years later, she described what it was like the day she found out. My biological father called her and told her that they needed to go to an important meeting. When she asked questions about where they were going and who they were meeting with, he wouldn't answer them. He drove her to the unmarked CPS building and took her inside, where a case worker presented the allegations and then handed her a signed statement where my biological father had admitted what he had done to me over the past three years. In an instant, sitting across from a stranger, in an undecorated office, in an unmarked building, my mom's world collapsed.

Until I survived a dysfunctional marriage myself, I didn't have a realistic picture of how dysfunction ingrains into the lives of everyone in its path, sabotaging healthy relationships and skewing the perception of normalcy. It's much easier to see how normal became distorted when looking back in hindsight, but in the middle of dysfunction, it's almost impossible to see. Dysfunction is like quicksand that sucks you under and makes it impossible to get out without help. I can't judge my mom from my perspective now because that wasn't her vantage point then. I truly, with all my heart believe that she would have gone to the ends of the earth to protect me had she known.

I think most people would have crumbled under the pressure, but through faith and strength, my mom led us out of trauma. Somehow, some way, she just figured it out. She did her best to teach us that forgiveness meant that we would let go of how his actions impacted us, but it did not relieve him of consequences. She taught us that allowing hatred, anger, and bitterness to remain in our lives would ultimately destroy us. She taught us to find forgiveness so we could move forward and heal. Our forgiveness was not so he could have peace; it was so we could.

When my mom found herself suddenly single after seventeen years of marriage, she was making less than $18,000 a year. Somehow, she made it stretch while raising three teenagers, keeping us in a stable house, paying for counseling, paying for sports, keeping the lights on, and putting food on the table. Although later, she would go on to teach herself computer skills and climb the corporate ladder, becoming the Director of Technology at a major hospital network, at that time, life was quite different.

I have never seen anyone try so hard to keep her family together. To this day, I still can't figure out how she made it all work, or how she kept us all grounded in Christ enough that we didn't all lose our minds. In the midst of raging trials and tragedies, she raised three children who all serve the Lord to this day, who all have successful careers, and who all love each other.

My older sister, Elicia, is a Master's level ABA Therapist, dedicated to her job and making a huge difference in the lives of children with Autism Spectrum disorders. She beat cancer—like totally rocked out her fight in an impressive way. She is her own person, unmoved by people's opinions of her or her choices, and I *love* her for it. She has blue hair, and she wears funky clothes that just work to create her own unique style. She is a southern gospel music enthusiast and has been since we were teens. She was the first person ever in our family, on three sides of our family, to earn a college degree. Not just one degree, but three of them. She loves fiercely and has a heart of gold. *She's kind of a big deal, y'all.*

My brother, Mathew, lives in Oklahoma with his beautiful wife and their six children. He is the Executive Director at his church. To join the church staff, he left a successful career in Corporate America where he worked his tail off to provide for his family and did a great job at it. One of my favorite things about Mathew being on the pastoral staff is that he gets to preach sometimes. When he was a baby, he was prophesied over by a traveling evangelist that came to our church. He said that my brother would preach one day and minister to a lot of people. The first time we turned on the television to watch him preach a service, we all cried. God did exactly what He said He would do. Mathew is an amazing father and has turned out to be a really great husband. Bless his wife's heart, most of his kids act at least a little like him, which means Heather is the Ring Master of a crazy, beautiful family circus. Together they are raising some of the coolest, most grounded kids I have ever met.

The weekend after Thanksgiving of 1993, my mom remarried. Terry Roberts and my mom had grown up together in church. He was someone that she knew, trusted, and had been friends with since she was 15. It didn't take long for their friendship to evolve into love. At the time, all I could think of was that it had only been six months since my biological father had passed away. I didn't like my first dad, and I was not about to give the new guy a chance to hurt me or my family.

While Terry could not have been prepared to step into a full-time bonus-dad role to three battle-scarred teenagers and their very wounded mother, he did it, and he did a great job at it. Of course, he had his own baggage, quirks, fears, and insecurities. It would take years of Terry consistently showing me that he was safe, and ultimately teaching us how a true father was supposed to be before he earned my trust, love, and respect.

Terry was kind, and he showed us unconditional, unfailing love, and more than anything else, he was steady. He didn't have pipedreams that he'd chase and move us from house to house like my biological father had done. Terry worked at the same job for many years until he retired. He got up at the same time every morning, ate the same breakfast most days, went to work on the same route, ate at Braum's for lunch before parking under the exact same tree to take a nap in his truck named Old Blue for the remainder of his lunch break. He stopped by the same Sonic on the way home to get a Dr. Pepper and got home pretty close to the same time every single day. He was consistent, he was solid, and he was faithful.

If he said he was going to do something, he did it. I knew exactly what would make him mad, like leaving the kitchen cabinets open, or messing with the thermostat. And I knew exactly what to expect when he was angry, like he might grumble and slam a cabinet door shut, but he absolutely would never hurt us. He was exactly who we needed in our lives. Today, I am so thankful God didn't answer my prayers to "just make him go away." God knew that we needed Terry in our lives. He chose to love us every single day, even though we didn't make that easy for him.

Terry had a daughter from a previous marriage, and despite my apprehension about having a new dad in my life, my bonus-sister Kim and I became instant friends the first time we met. She lived in Indiana with her mom where she had been raised. She came to Texas to visit her dad for a couple of weeks at Christmas and six weeks in the summer. Terry adored Kim, and very quickly, so did the rest of us.

Kim was the perfect addition to our family. Today, she is a Director at a hospital system in Indiana, married to the love of her life, Chris, and she is an amazing mom to two phenomenal children. She's kind and caring and supportive. She is stronger than she knows and watching her go through losing her mom to cancer recently was the hardest thing I have ever seen. Her mom was a true warrior and fought with grace. Kim has that same fighter spirit. We text and call each other almost daily. We have a tradition of thirty-second pep talks before we face something we are nervous about, like job interviews or up and coming speaking events. I can't imagine life without her. I am thankful she was part of the package deal when our parents got married.

After my son "Country" was born *(don't worry, it's a nickname)*, he and Terry had an instant bond. They are inseparable to this day. Over time, as Terry continued to silently prove himself, I let down my walls, and eventually I started calling him Dad. I have all the respect and love in the world for my dad and how he handled an incredibly difficult situation. When I say "my dad," I am always referring to Terry. He earned that right, even though back when he married my mom, I couldn't have predicted that he would hold such a special place in my heart.

Though I didn't recognize it at the time, when our bonus family formed, life as we all knew it changed for the better. I can't think of a single time that I have seen my parents fight. I hear stories from them about past disagreements, but it didn't happen in front of us. Of course, there were times they were united in anger at one of us kids, but for the most part, our house was much more peaceful. The term "step" was banished from our vocabulary from the beginning and could only be heard when I was being a super-brat.

It didn't take long to establish that family is family and that Kim was my sister as much as Elicia was. I inherited bonus aunts and uncles that loved me like they'd known me all of my life. I mean, they *had* known me most of my life because of church, but the level of love that they poured out on my siblings and I was beyond what I could have imagined. In our family, after you have come around a time or two, we pretty much adopt you in and claim you as one of our own. We established pretty early on that family is not defined by blood, but by love.

CHAPTER SIX

What I Do + How I Make Others Feel = Identity

I can't tell you how many times people have said to me that I should just forget about the past. If only it were that easy. No matter how hard I tried to leave my past behind me, the aftermath spilled over into a continual pattern of negative relationships and poor decision-making. Even though I would have sworn under oath that I had forgiven my biological father, the effects of his abuse somehow still held my future captive. I was bound with fear and hurt.

I spent most of my adolescence being an angry victim, wrought with guilt for telling about the abuse, and feeling like I was directly responsible for my biological father's suicide. I often lashed out in anger at my parents. I didn't make loving me very easy. Lucky for me, they loved me anyway. They loved me even when I blamed my mom for the abuse that she had no way of knowing about. They were patient with me even when I was a complete jerk to my dad for no other reason than the fact that he married my mom and he was in our lives. I was miserable at school because I felt like I had to pretend I was okay all the time. Youth Group was the one and only place I found refuge.

I wanted to be at church all the time. If the doors were opened, I insisted on being there. That worsened when I started dating one of the guys from church my sophomore year of high school. He looked past my flaws and saw something that he thought was beautiful, my heart. He accepted me as I was, and he excelled in giving me encouragement through words of affirmation. He told me I was beautiful, he said he loved me, he promised he would never hurt me, and that we would be together forever. We weren't. Our relationship lasted two years.

During that relationship I tested and crossed boundaries. I questioned my belief system and explored feelings and urges that I had never had before. He was my first in a lot of ways: my first real kiss, the first person I allowed myself to blindly trust, and the first person I gave my heart to. I was vulnerable, and there were parts of our relationship during the first 18 months that were innocent and sweet. He helped me find healing and listened to me as I told him all my secrets. I got a thrill out of the ways I could make him feel. We dreamed of a future together. The more he wanted to be with me, the more my self-worth soared.

As we continually pushed physical boundaries, eventually the topic of having sex came up. It didn't happen the first time we talked about it, or even the second, but eventually, I said yes. I remember a slow erosion of my resolve as I questioned whether I was ready or not, or if I was going against God's plan. There was a transition from "I'll wait until I am married" to little doubts of "Is it really wrong if I'm in a committed relationship?" I landed somewhere around "Where does the Bible *actually* say what is okay and what isn't?" Over time my views on sex were influenced a lot more by mainstream society than the Church. Frankly, nobody in the Church was talking about it, and *everybody* outside of the Church seemed to be doing it and thoroughly enjoying it. It became the forbidden fruit that I didn't understand why I couldn't have.

So, I said *yes*. I said *yes* because I thought it was the next step in a relationship. I believed that if I loved him, I'd show him. I wanted to have a sexual experience on my own terms. I said *yes* because I justified that it wouldn't be wrong if we got married later. After all, we were going to be together forever. Turns out, sex ruined everything. Giving myself to him that day felt good during the act, but afterward, we weren't prepared to handle the fallout. Honestly, I don't think that having sex too early was even the worst part of my decision, I think that it was way worse to convince myself that God was okay with it. Sex changes relationships. It isn't always a bad change, but something will change. For me and that guy, it changed a lot, because I said *yes* for all the wrong reasons.

Sex changed my relationship negatively because I wasn't at peace with my decision. I didn't know how to communicate that to my boyfriend. I didn't realize that I could have been honest and taken a step back. I could have said that I wanted to slow things down. I didn't say that. I shut down my heart and ran. I convinced myself that he never really loved me and that he wanted the same thing that I thought all men wanted: sex.

I had absolutely no idea what God's plan for sex was. I honestly didn't figure it out until I was in my thirties. At that point, I was at the beginning of a journey to get out of my own mind, and sex was an off-limits topic between me and God. I wasn't sure how He felt about sex, and I wasn't sure I wanted to know. I wasn't proud of my past choices, and I didn't know if God would ever want me because I didn't feel pure or clean. I didn't trust Him to handle the raw truth about the times I had given myself away, even though He knew the truth long before I confessed it. I allowed myself to believe that God viewed me how the older women in church had viewed me, as promiscuous. I had deep rooted church scars from my young adult days when people in the church called me a slut behind my back, and not much better to my face.

Unbeknownst to me at the time, God's view of me was drastically different than what was conveyed in the harsh messages of people who really didn't know me. I didn't realize that God still had a plan to make me whole. I had no idea that He could restore me and that I could be completely pure in His eyes. I was shocked to realize that I could talk about sex with God, pray about purity, and ask Him to show me His plan without feeling shame. What so many people who criticized or judged me failed to realize was how much my identity was intertwined with my sexuality. People blamed my past and touted that I should "forgive and forget" or "let go and let God." My problem wasn't that I hadn't forgiven my biological father. It was how his betrayal crocheted my self-worth into my ability and willingness to please men to the point that I couldn't separate the two without totally unravelling. I felt obligated to provide physical pleasure when a man expressed desire in me. I had no idea that I had the right to say *no*, nor that I could say *no* and still be safe. The more situations that I was in where sex was expected of me, the more I believed that it was a requirement for love.

The dangerous perception I adopted was that my whole purpose in life was to please people. The potential for negative consequences were endless, and they prevented healing. In order to take control of my sexuality, I had to establish a positive connotation trigger with the word *no*. In my mind, *no* was the scariest word in the English language. I knew that when I said *yes* to something or someone, even if I didn't want to do what they asked or expected, I could predict what would happen next. I would do what was asked and pretend to be happy about it. They would be happy that I did it, and life would go on. I would be the only one who knew that I didn't want to do whatever it was. However, I feared that telling people *no* would evoke an unpredictable emotional response. *No* could endanger my safety or end a relationship.

Developing a positive connotation trigger with the word *no* meant that I had to view myself as worthy, brave, and courageous. I had to learn that I had the right to say *no*, that a man's erection wasn't my responsibility to fix, and that it was okay to speak up when I didn't like something. I learned that there wasn't a point of no return; I could stop a sexual experience at any time. If it was hurting me, if I changed my mind, or if it just didn't feel how I thought it should feel, I had every right to say that I wanted to stop. I also had to learn that I had the right to experience pleasure and fulfillment. Perhaps most importantly, I had to learn that I was worth waiting for until I was ready and that I didn't owe it anyone to have sex with them.

There were a few other truths I had to discover, like the fact that sex wouldn't make someone stay if they wanted to go, or that I didn't have to have sex with someone out of fear that they'd leave me for someone who would. A lot of my misguided decisions were rooted in wanting to be loved and accepted by someone, by anyone. While I was floating on butterflies and rainbows when I met someone new, I compromised beliefs, boundaries, and values.

From my earliest memories when I was just seven years old, the message I internalized about sex was that it was not about what I wanted, rather it happened when a man wanted me. I honestly believed that if I wasn't offering sex to a man, then he had absolutely no reason to keep me around. I viewed my contribution to the relationship as incomplete without physical intimacy. I spent many years attempting to become the ideal "perfect girlfriend" that I had concocted in my head based on conversations with men, watching movies, and listening to song lyrics.

My misguided beliefs positioned me to let others use me and then go on with their life to do whatever they wanted without any questions from me. I made myself available without boundaries. In my mind, being the perfect girlfriend meant forcing myself not to care what they did when they weren't with me. I never asked questions like, "Where is this going?" or, "Where were you. I thought we had plans?" I avoided anything that would be deemed as clingy or needy. I gave myself away and asked for absolutely nothing in return, secretly wishing that they would care about me enough to offer themselves back to me, but never once asking for it, or valuing myself enough to demand it.

BOND with me here. My abused heart and mind led me into relationships with men whose views of me mirrored my own, and whose abusive words mirrored the emotionally abusive insults I heaped upon myself. I didn't find myself worthy of a commitment. I thought I was too broken, too messed up, too heavy, too ugly, that I didn't make enough money, wasn't as healthy as I wanted to be, wasn't successful enough, wasn't talented enough, or maybe the worst lie I believed—that I just wasn't the "forever girl." I accepted what I thought I could get as a consolation prize because I didn't believe that I deserved what I wanted. Beyond just having partners that I wished I hadn't, or experiences that I wished I had avoided, I also had smaller regrets like participating in conversations that went beyond my comfort zone without having the courage to say I was uncomfortable. Some of my deepest wounds came from relationships that I allowed to be entirely sexual in nature when what I really wanted was intimacy and commitment.

I was raised in a time when a lot of people treated sex as if it were the unpardonable sin. "Absolutely not!" was the only appropriate answer to anything involving sexual temptation. While it's true that the Bible tells us to flee when it comes to temptation, He does have a plan for us to have and enjoy healthy sexual relationships. God never intended sex and intimacy to be tied to guilt and shame. Somewhere along the way, we made it the sin to beat all sins and decided its offenders were banishment-worthy.

At nineteen, when I lived with my grandmother, my teenage cousin came home from school asking what oral sex was. *Okay, she used a much more graphic term that she heard on the school bus from an older boy, and when she said that word, my grandmother almost passed out in the dining room floor.* To make matters worse, I turned to my cousin and answered her question. She responded with, "Ewww! Gross! I would never want to do that!" I replied, "Exactly! You aren't ready to talk about sex with nasty little boys."

When my grandmother got angry with me, I explained, "She either learns the truth at home, where it is safe to ask questions, or the little boy on the bus who taught her that word is going to answer her questions in a very different way than you'd want him to." Even back then, I knew that if we refused to talk about sex openly or create safe environments that foster learning, then we would also forfeit the right to control the narrative. Our thoughts and opinions become obsolete when we refuse to voice them.

CHAPTER SEVEN

You Can't Defy Gravity

From my own experiences, I developed a desire to help others in the Church learn about sexuality in a healthy, Godly way. After learning that I could be both Christian and human, I was able to develop a healthy connotation about the concept of sex and God's plan for it. In working with my clients, the topic of sex often comes up as a roadblock in people's lives because it can be a source of shame, regret, or insecurity for them. I have learned to set aside my personal convictions, as well as my own thoughts, opinions, and judgements, so I can hold mutually openminded conversations free of preconceived notions. By keeping the dialogue open and honest, I am able to answer questions and help identify sexual scars for men and women who wish more than anything that they could rewind time and erase some of their past choices.

I often think about how we as a Church can better equip people to navigate healthy and safe decisions grounded in God's plan. What if we taught young people to look forward to a time when they can have a meaningful and fulfilling sexual relationship, ordained by God, with a partner they have vowed to explore pleasure with for the rest of their life? What if that was our approach instead of, "Don't do it! Don't talk about it! Don't think about it! Don't look at it. Just don't!" What if we explained consequences, beyond pregnancy, to help people decide if they are ready for the responsibilities and repercussions of adult decisions?

I want people who feel they have made poor choices in their past to understand that there is nothing too dirty or shameful to be redeemed by Christ. I want to talk about it because there is real emotion tied up in this. When I ask clients to choose one word to describe their sexual experiences, their word is rarely positive. The top answers that I get include shame, hurt, trauma, regret, fear, insecurity, and feeling lost. Other clients have told me that they simply don't understand why God cares what they do with their own body.

God does care about our sexuality because God cares about our heart and soul. When two people become one flesh their spirits unite. He cares about who we allow to become a part of us forever. We live in a sex-crazed world. Sex is on commercials, TV shows, and movies. It's in music lyrics, dance moves, and the books we read. Sex in media is not limited to overt pornography, strip clubs, and prostitutes; those are outlets that stem from sexual addictions. In our everyday lives we are exposed to sexual images and innuendos hundreds of times a day. I believe that's because sex is the only experience a non-believer can have that creates a moment of spiritual satisfaction. Though it may be fleeting, there is a surge of elation that transpires all the way down to their soul the moment their spirit collides with another person's spirit. It's kind of like a spiritual defibrillator.

Here's the problem, sexual unity isn't optional. Every time I gave myself away, unity happened whether I wanted it to or not. I gave pieces of my soul away as souvenirs to unworthy tourists who were only passing through my life. Without thinking about the consequences, without considering what state their spirit was in, I unintentionally invited their spirit to connect with mine. Even when I told myself that it was all physical, I couldn't take the spiritual aspect of it away. I could turn off my mind, I could even shut down my emotions, but I could not remove the spiritual component of sex. I couldn't change or break spiritual law any more than I could defy gravity. It was beyond my control. Past partners became a part of me, and they took a part of me with them when they left my life.

Thankfully God is *Jehovah Rapha*, "the God who heals me." He created a new wholeness in me. He purified me and made me complete again when I came to Him a completely broken mess. I couldn't rewind time or undo my past decisions. I couldn't get my innocence back. It was the ultimate price I paid for the choices I had made. The consequences of having sex are lifelong. It gets messy quickly when I think about the potential state of past partner's souls. If their soul was a compilation of their original form, intertwined and blended with the people they had united with, then in truth, I had no way of knowing who I was creating soul ties with. God knew. He knew exactly what I was getting involved with, and that's precisely why He cares about my sexuality.

When I think about God's plan for sex, how thoughtful He was in His creativity and His perfect plan for our bodies, I consider how God created women's bodies to bleed the first time they have sex, creating a blood covenant with their first partner. There is Biblical significance in blood covenants. In Biblical times, a blood covenant represented an unbreakable oath between two people. When someone desired to bond with another person who wasn't connected to them by DNA, they took a blood covenant oath, meaning they cut themselves and meshed the wounds together, exchanging blood. The oath represented something deep inside of them that could not be extracted. They could never go back and separate blood from blood to indicate "this is mine, and that is yours."

Let's BOND for a minute. We can break up, move on, disavow, divorce, or separate, but there is a part of us that we don't get to take back, the part we left behind in a blood covenant. I changed my lifestyle when I realized that I was a compilation of the souls I had picked up along the way and was in essence regifting myself to everyone I connected with. It made total sense to me why I felt spiritually empty. I had left pieces of myself with people I shouldn't have. My entire walk with God changed when I started making healthier sexual decisions. I was able to move forward because I had been forgiven and restored through God's healing power and grace. I finally realized that I was carrying anger, hurt, and hatred for my exes over cheating, leaving, and wounds based on years of abuse and neglect. But by hating someone who was a part of me, I was hating a part of myself. What I was feeling was less about losing a part of myself that they took with them, and more about the uncertainty of what to do with what they left behind.

As I began to reconcile my relationship with God, it made sense that it had to start with my sexual identity. I needed spiritual healing, and that had to start with spiritual wholeness. When I went before God, I had to truly lay my past at His feet. I had to cling to His willingness to purify me. Our brains were not designed to forget. Sometimes I had to forgive myself over and over because every time I remembered my past experiences, shame consumed me all over again. God doesn't work like that, though. When God looked my repentant heart, He forgave me completely and totally. He let go of the choices

I made and completely restored me into fellowship with Him. My relationship with Him was without blemish. God's plan for my life was always purity, and even though I had made choices that I wasn't proud of, God redeemed me. He made me whole again.

CHAPTER EIGHT

I Got a Prophetic Word

from a Drug Dealer

Four letters: S-L-U-T. That terrible combination of letters is all it took for me to leave the Church completely when I was eighteen years old. Even now that word brings me to tears. As a teenager with a boyfriend in a conservative church congregation, many assumptions were made about me, none of which were true. That word was spoken about me by people who didn't even know me. They really didn't know anything about me. That word, more than any other word I have heard in my whole life, wounded me the deepest.

BOND with me here. Our words have power. We can choose to speak life or destroy it. Never once, in all the times when someone criticized my virtue, did I ever turn and thank them for bringing it to my attention. It did not spark a beautiful revelation nor send me to my knees ready to repent and make a life change. Quite the opposite, I felt hurt and misunderstood. I felt judged and rejected. Every time someone said something cruel, I took one step further out the door of the Church.

I turned eighteen in September of 1997, my senior year of high school. I thought that I was ready to be out in the world on my own. Like many young people teetering between teen years and adulthood, I didn't want anyone to enforce rules or hold me accountable to healthy boundaries. No matter how much my parents loved me, I continued to push them away. I held onto anger and resentment that grew the more I felt misunderstood. I withheld trust from everyone around me and adopted an "I'll reject you before you reject me" mindset. Feeling rejected and worthless, I made a decision to leave my home, my church, my friends, and everyone who cared about me, vowing that if that was who God was, and that was what love was, then I wanted nothing to do with it.

I moved out of my parents' house at the beginning of my senior year and finished my whole senior curriculum in three weeks at a district program for seniors who were at risk of not graduating. Nobody expected me to finish so quickly, but I tested out of most of my classes and whipped through the rest. I stayed with friends for a while, then I got my own apartment long before I was ready.

There was a teen dance club in Arlington where I began to branch out of my upbringing and into a world I knew nothing about. It was the first time I remember guys overtly making advances towards me. I discovered that I could actually dance and enjoyed it. It was at that club that I met the young man who would later become my first husband. We met in December, and in February he shipped out to Boot Camp in the Great Lakes for the US Navy. Two months isn't long for a whirlwind romance, but I thought I was head over heels in love with him, and I vowed to "stay by his side always." *So much for writing off love forever.*

It was during that time that I began to push the boundaries in my life to unrecognizable limits. I took a job at a gentleman's club. I don't think any single decision I have made in my life since going to work at that club caused as big of a rift with my family as that did. I justified working at the club with the facts that I was just a waitress and all of my clothes stayed on, but my family was not buying it. If I am being honest with myself, I would admit that there were lifelong impacts of working in that environment. There were fun times, and I experienced a thrill when men would tell me I was beautiful or buy me a drink. Only, I didn't really drink.

I didn't have my first taste of alcohol until my twenty-first birthday. I grew up behind Miller Brewery and knew only two things about beer: it smells like pee, and I never wanted to taste it. I still have never tasted it! I also had a close family member who was an alcoholic and saw it destroy his life. I knew I was the type of person who would get hooked on something quickly. I envisioned myself as the girl who tried drugs once and became addicted. So, I never tried drugs, not even marijuana, because I was terrified of addiction. I figured that I couldn't get addicted to something that I never tried.

So, unlike many of my underage friends who got wasted every night, I didn't drink at all. The bartender made me fake drinks that looked like the real deal but didn't contain alcohol. I pretended to drink with the customers because it got me better tips, and we weren't allowed to turn a customer down when they offered to buy us drinks. Most of the time, it didn't bother me, but there were people that I didn't want to sit down and have a drink with. I didn't have that option. Most of my customers were friendly men who just came to the club to have fun with their friends. I met famous athletes, wealthy businessmen, film producers, and a few random celebrities. There were also the jerks and the creeps. Customers don't have to pass a background check to be admitted, and the nature of a gentleman's club doesn't exactly invite actual gentlemen. There were felons and sex offenders and guys who took advantage of the fact that they could degrade women without consequences.

While working there, I pushed the boundaries of what I could learn about sex because I thought it would make me the "best girlfriend ever." I felt deeply insecure and inadequate when it came to sex. I felt like I had both been exposed early, but also that I didn't know anything about sex in the way that other women in the club knew. The dancers adopted me as their little sister and always had plenty of advice to offer about my dating life.

I constantly compared myself to others and battled body image. I developed a full-fledged eating disorder, going days, and sometimes weeks at a time, without food. I developed a warped sense of what men wanted, and my views of men became further skewed by the population that frequented the club.

I had a manager who was kind to me. One night after work, he asked me to drive him home. I did. On the way there, he told me about the drug problems he had gotten himself into. The police had seized a lot of his assets and they were closing in on him as a large-scale dealer and manufacturer. At first, I just thought he was oversharing. I didn't understand why he was opening up to me. Then when we got to his house, he said thank you and gave me the strangest look. He paused for what felt like a long time, but it was probably only awkward seconds. Then he asked, "What church did you grow up in?" I was shocked. I didn't answer him, but looked down, feeling a sense of shame. He went on to explain that he was a preacher's kid. He had grown up in church and strayed far away from it. Then he said something I hope I never forget. "You don't belong here, Andi, and you can't stay here too much longer, or it will change you forever. God has a plan for your life, and this isn't it. You are supposed to change the world." Talk about the unexpected, I actually got a word from God from a drug dealer. I never saw him again after that night.

What I didn't know at the time, and wouldn't for several years, is what was happening outside of the club before my manager asked me to take him home. That night my mom and dad drove to the club. Dad wouldn't let her go inside to get me, but she had been outside of the club praying over me, walking around my car, and praying over my life. She was calling me home in spiritual warfare. She prayed over my safety and that God would send someone to speak life into me who could reach me in a way that I would hear them. Turns out, that someone was a drug dealer. God can use *anyone*.

Working at the club changed after that conversation with my manager. I wish I could say that I had an instant transformation, or that I was miraculously inspired to fix my life, but that wasn't how it happened. My life situation got much worse before it got better, but the words my manager spoke over me planted a seed that would grow eventually. There would be many times in my future that I would remember sitting in my car that night, surrounded by darkness, and the "what just happened" silence that ensued as soon as the door closed behind my manager, and he trotted up the path to his house. I experienced a pivotal transition.

I became restless, mostly because I wasn't living my life in a way that was true to my core values. I tried to ease my restlessness by running harder and faster from anyone who knew my story. I tried moving to Detroit with a friend

I met at the club, and that lasted all of six weeks. When I came back, I moved in with my grandmother in East Texas.

CHAPTER NINE

The Tangled Web of Lies

My boyfriend came home on military leave for a couple of weeks in the summer of 1999. I felt "off" the whole time he was home. I thought maybe it was shame because I had been with another guy. I felt incredibly guilty about it—not guilty enough to be honest with him or anyone else, but guilty enough to lie, and to keep lying until I was in a huge mess. The whole time he was home, I battled nausea and exhaustion. I just didn't feel like myself. I chalked it up to a combination of Texas summer heat and stress. At that time, I wasn't eating, so I often felt nauseated when I was around food. My menstrual cycles were basically nonexistent, so I wasn't alarmed when I missed a few periods.

My boyfriend and I both knew that our relationship had changed. We had an amicable breakup the night before he left. I spent the night with him, drove him to the airport, and said what I thought would be our final goodbye. Later that day, I finally gave in and talked to a friend about the physical symptoms I'd been experiencing. Glynda immediately drove to the store, bought a pregnancy test, and headed to my house. I took the test while we waited nervously. Before I even sat the test on the counter, two lines appeared. I was pregnant.

In what was supposed to be the happiest moment of my life, I only felt terrified. I knew I wasn't ready to be a mom; I was a mess! I looked at myself and saw a girl who made terrible choices, worked for minimum wage, cheated on her boyfriend, got pregnant, had an eating disorder, and lied to everyone about all of it. None of that seemed like mom material. The day I found out I was pregnant with my son, I hadn't eaten in twenty-three days. I believed that I wasn't the type of woman my child would be proud to call *Mom*.

I actually have a few BOND moments about my pregnancy and early stages of being a mother. First, with the disclaimer that I was at a very different place in my life, I will say that I didn't know for the first few months whether or not I was going to keep my pregnancy. For a couple of weeks, I contemplated abortion before deciding that I just couldn't live with that decision. Even back then, when I had stepped pretty far away from my faith, I knew in my heart that there would be lifelong emotional consequences of regret, guilt, and shame if I chose that route.

I also considered adoption. Actually, I heavily considered adoption. I looked into going to live at the Gladney Adoption Center in Fort Worth. I ultimately decided that while I wasn't ready yet, I would spend the next six months trying to get ready. I bought every parenting book I could find and studied parenting like a college class. I had a solid support system surrounding me, but in all honesty, I didn't do everything the right way.

Confession: I made some really terrible decisions around that pregnancy that impacted my son and his father forever. I was terrified and made a selfish, stupid decision to tell my son's father that Country wasn't his, and I chose to move home to my parents and raise Country alone. At the time, I truly, misguidedly, believed I was making the best decision for all parties involved, only I didn't have the right to make that decision alone. I thought Country's dad wasn't ready to be a father, *ironic since I also thought I wasn't ready to be a mother*. I was a year older than Country's dad, and I truly felt like I was letting him off the hook of having a baby early. In my mind, I was releasing him to start his own life and do whatever he wanted to do with it. I reasoned that if he wanted our son, then he'd fight for him. I replayed the words of the counselors from my childhood saying, "You were abused. You are going to marry an abuser." I don't know if I made my decisions out of fear, selfishness, or pity, but ultimately, I decided to lie, and I took his right to be in his son's life away.

They both missed six years of each other because I took it upon myself to fix something that wasn't mine to fix. I couldn't take it back. No amount of apologizing or wishing it hadn't happened could erase the lie I told. While I owned up to the lie with my son, and my son's father was pretty forgiving, it didn't take away the consequential impact that my choice had on others, and I couldn't make that go away.

I will say that from the time Country was born, even now as he is a twenty-year-old man, I try to be the best mom to him that I know how to be. In some ways, we grew up together. Even though my life as a mom got off to a misguided start, being a good mom became the mission that I could not be deterred from. I didn't always make the best choices. Country and I have been through hell and back together. Sometimes I wasn't as consistent with him as I should have been. I failed at being a good provider and moved him around way too often. However, I can look back on my time as a mom with pride.

I can say that I taught Country to pursue his dreams, and I taught him to be a good person. I raised him to have a strong belief system and to be a man of integrity. I put mentors in his life to help guide him as he became a Godly man. I prayed over him daily. I was fiercely protective, and maybe a bit helicopter-y, but anyone who was around us knew that I loved him with every ounce of my heart, and that I would have gone to the ends of the earth to make sure he had everything he needed in life, and most of what he wanted.

I wish I could say that getting pregnant and lying to my son's father was the only time that I tried to overcorrect in life. But I had a habit of fixing bad decisions with more bad decisions, which for obvious reasons, didn't work out in my favor. Country's dad wasn't the only person I lied to during that time. I had so many different stories going, it was hard to keep them all straight. I continued to perpetuate the cycle of poor decision-making for years.

CHAPTER TEN

Being A Military Wife On 9/11

The year 2000 kicked off a new century for the world, and a new life for me. I had Country that year and learned another valuable lesson: breakups are not always forever. The breakup from the night before I found out I was pregnant didn't last. The First (husband) and I had broken up because he admitted to me that he was still in love with his ex-girlfriend, and I encouraged him to see what was there. I honestly felt like it was the best option for him. I wasn't devastated about the breakup because I didn't see myself as the kind of girl that was supposed to be in someone's life forever. I had accepted that people left and that I was only in people's lives for a season. When he expressed feelings towards his ex, I was the first to say that he should explore it and find peace.

After he flew back to the base, he called me and expressed appreciation that it took a lot of love for me to put his needs before my own. He wanted to give us another try. I told him about the pregnancy, but I weaved in lies with the truth. Those lies cracked the foundation of our marriage, and we would never be able to move past them because in his heart, despite my every protest, he knew I wasn't being completely honest. The truth wrapped in a lie was still a lie. It was still a distortion of facts, and it became the ticking timebomb ready to destroy my marriage upon explosion.

I was still completely obsessed with The First, and I confused codependency for true love. I thought that being with him forever was the realization of my childhood dreams, and I was willing to do absolutely anything to make that happen. I didn't care who I lost or what I compromised, I wanted one thing and that was to be his wife. I knew he didn't love me like I loved him. I knew that he cared about me, that we had a beautiful friendship, but as far as being deeply, madly in love with me, that wasn't him. I believed that I could love deeply enough for both of us, and I thought we'd figure the rest out along way.

We married on my twenty-first birthday and two months later, Country and I moved from Texas to a small military community two hours north of Seattle. The marriage was shaky from the beginning. As we changed and grew apart, we fought more frequently. He went out with his friends more; I retreated more. I had better computer skills than I let on, and I quickly discovered his email passwords. Obsessively, I would read email exchanges between him and other women. I didn't confront him because I didn't want to give it away that I had his passwords. I gave the illusion that I trusted him, but I didn't. Every email I saw made me try harder in all the wrong ways to capture his attention and keep it.

I tried to fix our relationship with intimacy and quality time. I tried lavishing words of affirmation on him and complimenting him constantly. However, the problem was that I had started the marriage with a lie and that lie caused huge cracks in the foundation of our relationship. I never repaired those cracks in the foundation, I just tried to change and rebuild without ever fixing the damage. It was not enough to just build a new structure on the same broken foundation. The structure of my marriage was never stable because it was built on a broken foundation.

There were many other problems, all of which would have caused problems on their own, but when combined with a major foundation problem, ultimately caused the collapse of my marriage. I didn't know how to create peace in my home because I didn't have peace in my life. I didn't have a reference point that would indicate that I was doing it all wrong. I was messy. I didn't even try to cook out of fear of failing at it. I didn't know how to manage money. I hid my weaknesses, faults, and insecurities, and tried to constantly portray the image that I was okay. I wasn't. I needed serious counseling to deal with my past, and to open up about the lies I told, and why. I believed that if I ever started telling the truth, everything would crumble around me. It did crumble, but it was definitely not because I told the truth.

My tunnel vision was a huge problem. My unwillingness to be honest and confront issues was a chasm between us. I was ultra-clingy and the more I clung to him, the less he wanted me. I was suffocating him. There was never a time where he could just exist in his own home without someone needing something from him. He began to seek solace in other places. I believed that if I only loved him more, then it would fix everything. Only, no matter how hard I tried, I couldn't love enough for both of us. My words and thoughts demonstrated that I loved him fiercely, but my actions drove us apart.

To make matters worse, he was in the Navy and was doing workups for cruise. That meant that he was home a week and gone a week, and then home a week and gone two weeks, gradually increasing until his six-month deployment on an aircraft carrier. The crew headed out for the six-month deployment at the end of Summer 2001, and on Tuesday morning, September 11, we were emailing each other back and forth.

I was devoted to my family, without question. I balanced my whole life around Country and The First. I adjusted my sleep schedule to be available when The First could email or call, no matter what time of day that might be. Mid-conversation on September 11, 2001, I received an urgent email from him that said he didn't know when we'd talk again. Something had happened that he couldn't discuss, and communication was being shut down on the ship. I sat in a panic staring at the words "I love you," not knowing what to do next. My panic escalated when I turned on the TV in time to see the second plane hit the World Trade Center. I watched in horror as the Towers fell. My husband was on the ship that pulled into position to launch the first air attacks.

I was terrified for the next six months. Well-meaning friends and family checked in to make sure he was safe. I received frequent calls with rumors and news reports about bombings of our military ships. Every time I got a call, I grew anxious until I heard from other wives, or on rare occasion, when I got to hear from my husband. He couldn't tell me where he was or what was happening with the War on Terrorism. One day I received a Time magazine in the mail that had the location of our ships on the cover. I fell to the floor crying in complete hysteria. I couldn't know where my husband was, but the press published it for the world to see? My husband's carrier was clearly listed on the front cover, and I viewed it as a threat to his safety.

When he got home, his duty station had changed to Corpus Christi, Texas. We settled in together, but things were never really okay between us. We did a great job parenting Country together, and had amazing moments, but our relationship was far from healthy. I had my first miscarriage in Corpus Christi. I became depressed and made my first and only actual suicide attempt the day I lost the baby. I never told anybody about the pills I took after leaving the doctor that day. I was shocked and angry when I woke up and the emotional pain was more than I thought I could endure.

My self-worth was wrapped up in my ability to please, and I couldn't please my husband, I couldn't make him happy, and I couldn't give him a baby. He loved Country, and they were really close, but we both wanted more kids. During my depression, our marriage got worse. He often left at night to go out with his friends. I would put Country to bed, and then spend hours sitting in the bay window on the second story of our townhome, watching for his car to come down the road. Sometimes it wouldn't turn into the parking lot until ten or eleven the next morning. I pretended like I didn't care, but my eyes were swollen, and my voice was hoarse from crying all night.

I sought the counsel of my pastor. His fearless feedback was that I had to establish boundaries in my life. I had to let The First know that I wanted him to stay, but only if he wanted to be there. Wanting to be there came with actions, not just words. It looked like coming home at night. It looked like communicating with each other. It looked like working on our marriage together. I tried to do that, but still, the problems got worse.

The more I felt rejected by him, the more I gave up. I didn't do the one thing he needed me to do: be honest with him. He came home one night at two or three in the morning, got in bed beside me, but didn't say a word. We faced opposite directions. Tears ran down my face as I said, "I am moving back home to my mom's." I was defeated. I don't remember if he responded or not. I think in some ways he was relieved. I cried a lot while packing up our stuff to move six hours back home to my parents. I can remember sitting on the floor of our townhouse feeling like my soul was being torn in two.

BOND with me here? It would be easy to justify divorce on the grounds that I had proof he was cheating. I had email proof of recaps where he had spent "amazing nights" with another woman. I could have been resentful, but that wouldn't help me grow. If I look back at 2002 with full transparency and honesty, I have to also accept the fact that I played a 50% role in the failing of my marriage. I lied, shut down, clung, cried *a lot*, and ultimately backed him into a corner without the willingness to see his point of view. What he did was wrong, but I had a lot of wrongdoing in there as well.

When I left, I knew I was making the right decision. I needed to establish and enforce boundaries that would engender mutual respect and open communication. He was facing his own internal battles, and we were unable to find common ground. Divorce was hard, but it was almost a relief to have closure to the slow, agonizing death of our marriage. When I packed my son up in the moving truck, and headed back to Burleson, I felt deep grief. I grieved the loss of my marriage and of my idealistic image of how our family was supposed to be. I lost my happily ever after, and it hurt.

CHAPTER ELEVEN

The Princeless Princess

During my early twenties, I held onto a princess-mentality and clung to the expectation that one day my Prince Charming would magically appear and rescue me from the craziness that had been my life. I completely bought into the lie that "I'm incomplete, and he will complete me." Every fairy tale I had seen at that time, featured a damsel in distress just waiting for her prince to come. I was the princess, sitting in my tower, looking out over life as it passed me by, just dreaming of the day when my knight in shining armor would arrive on the scene, whisk me away, and save the day. We would share true love's first kiss, and then we would live happily ever after.

I bought into the lie that my perfect guy, my soul mate, would choose me, and I would just accept him and be grateful that he chose me. I feel a little silly admitting that I didn't understand that I had the power to choose the people who were in my life and the role that I allowed them to take in my life. So, I fell for the first guy who came around and seemed willing to rescue me, bonus points if he told me I was beautiful. I clung to a misconception cocktail that was equal parts fairy tale, chick flick, and romance novel. With all my heart I believed it could happen for me. I was looking for a fairy tale ending, which meant I drifted toward whatever felt good, whatever sounded good, and whomever painted a picture of a happy future together.

The fairy tale never included a divorce. It didn't include being a single mom again or reclaiming the starring role in my life's feature film, *The Princeless Princess*. It was time for plan B, and I'm not really a plan B kind of person. Plan B for me was to go back and make plan A work. Try again. Figure it out. That wasn't one of my options, though. I had to learn how to fall, then get back up, dust off, and move forward. It wasn't easy.

For a while, I drove Country to Corpus Christi almost every weekend, clinging to hope that my marriage would work out and our family would be put back together again. The more I went and saw how my ex-husband had moved on with his life, the further I stepped away from our marriage. I felt rejected and replaced. I eventually gave up hope, and rather than face loneliness, I solved the problem by meeting someone new. My heart wasn't ready for another relationship. The rebound wasn't healthy. We called it a Godly relationship because we had Biblically-based physical boundaries and prayed together, but it started before my divorce was final, which meant it was not time for a new relationship yet. That's where I learned that healthy doesn't come from broken. Two broken people do not equal a healthy relationship. That math doesn't add up. The relationship lasted a few months and then ended without drama. It just wasn't time yet.

After accepting that I needed time to heal, I took my first corporate job and started rebuilding my relationship with God. I dedicated a year of my life to abstaining from any type of dating relationships to ensure that I had time to heal and focus on the two most important priorities in my life: my son and God. I returned to the church I'd grown up in and volunteered in the Children's Ministry, eventually serving as the Children's Pastor.

Life seemed to be going great, and I was discovering a new normal. As I began to learn who I was as a person, separate from relationships or how others viewed me, I offered myself love and acceptance for the first time. Because dating wasn't an option, I opened my heart and mind to friendship without fear of ulterior motives.

Then, there was a huge setback. I had become close friends with a young man at church; we had grown up together and had always been friendly. I thought we were really close, but I didn't know as much about him as I thought I did. I didn't know he had a girlfriend, which wouldn't have mattered to me. Even though I wasn't trying to date him, it mattered to a lot of other people. Old Friend really liked Country, who was around four years old at the time. One day, Old Friend was complimenting my son's manners, and mentioned that "when I look at your son, I feel like I am looking at my son. I feel connected to him." I thought it was the coolest thing ever. I thought that God had placed a mentor in my son's life.

However, Old Friend mentioned his statement to one of the church leaders, who told him that he should be careful of me. The leader accused me of using my son to try to woo my friend and trap him into a relationship. He told my friend that I was trying to come between him and his girlfriend—*the girlfriend I didn't know about.* In some ways, I truly wish my friend hadn't told me what was said as he was explaining why he had to take a step back from our friendship and that our friendship was causing problems with his girlfriend. I was crushed. I felt betrayed by the church leader. I felt falsely accused and blindsided. It was awful.

I was caught off guard by that church scar. Mostly because I volunteered at least 10 hours every week, funded the entire children's ministry out of my pocket, and asked nothing in return. I didn't *want* anything in return, I just wanted to serve God and serve His church. Driven by the power of disappointment, I found myself taking a step back out the door of the Church. I didn't leave immediately, but it was the first step. I can trace back a deep-rooted church scar to that moment to identify a foundational crack that I had to go back and repair and it tied back to that same church scar from being called a slut in that same church.

I am not, by any means blaming the church, nor the leader, for my decisions after that event, but I recognize that it was a setback for me. I didn't handle it in the best way. I was wounded, filled with shame and anger, and a part of me gave up on churches all together. Instead of pouring my heart out to God or confronting the church leaders, I ran again. The walls around my heart were miles high and the deep wounds I carried kept me from considering the possibility of serving in ministry again for many years.

I found myself spiritually homeless and searching for validation. Feeling rejected by the church community I served, I sought the only other validation I had ever felt in my life, dating. Once again, I rejected love. I determined that I didn't need a church to have a relationship with God. I didn't really question God, but I questioned a lot of His people. However, the longer I was out of church, the more I slipped into old habits of making terrible decisions.

CHAPTER TWELVE

I Failed...Again

When my heart was hurting and I walked away from the church I was serving, I deeply wanted to go back to a simpler time in my life. Any time I have craved honest simplicity, it has taken back to the place I called home all of my life. Even though I grew up in Burleson, my roots were in Palestine. Mema and Papa lived on a 49-acre farm tucked back in the tall East Texas Pines of Swanson Hill, outside of Palestine. June 2, 1990, they decided to take trip to Burleson to see my family. They wanted to pick up my sister and take her back to the farm for a few weeks during the summer. All three of us kids rotated weeks as much as possible.

The trip started out normally. Mema always fell asleep before their car ever got off the blacktop road. Papa turned on the radio, set the cruise control to 55, and hit the highway on a trip they had made more than a time or two. Less than an hour into their drive, Papa fell asleep at the wheel, crossed the median and hit a cement culvert. He died in the Care Flite while en route to the hospital. Mema spent months in ICU and even longer in rehab. The only bones she didn't break were the ones in her face; all of the others were shattered. Most doctors didn't think she would survive, but she did. She wasn't supposed to walk or play the piano again, but she defied the odds.

She was best friends with Country's paternal great-grandmother, and it wounded her deeply that I wouldn't say out loud what everyone already knew: who Country's dad was. The last time I saw Mema, she was in the hospital following a mild stroke in 2005. In what would be her last request to me ever, she asked me to put our families back together. She passed away on Country's sixth birthday in 2006. Her funeral became the first time my son would lay eyes on his dad. After the funeral, I went back home. God put it on my heart to trust Him and that He would take care of everything. Country's aunt reached out to me in kindness and gently encouraged me to let Country meet his dad. I set aside my fear that Country's dad would take him away from me, knowing that in all actuality, he had every right to.

Country's dad was married. They had a three-year-old son and six-week-old baby girl. Fortunately, my son's father had given his wife a heads up that he thought Country was his son, and they expected to meet him one day, but thought it would be much later in Country's life when he chose to do that on his own. So, while it was a shock, it wasn't earth-shattering. I scheduled a meeting with my son's father and bonus mom. There were not words to fix what I had done. The apology felt cheap and worthless in comparison to taking away his opportunity to be a part of our son's life for his first six years. Thankfully they were kind and forgiving. We had a conversation that was six years overdue. I gave Country's dad the option of being in his life if he wanted to. I let him know that I would take full accountability for my decisions and answer any questions Country asked about never meeting his dad, but they never really came up.

Country had been praying for a dad every night for two years. He wanted a dad who looked just like him, and his prayers were very specific about that. God certainly answered those prayers, Country and his dad look exactly alike! The day they met, Country's six-week-old sister was in the hospital, but his dad didn't want to wait to meet him. I drove him to Palestine and explained to him that he was going to meet his dad. I openly confessed to my son that I had told a lie, and that lies hurt people. I told him that I had done a bad thing, but that I wanted to make it right. He patted the tears on my face and told me it'd be okay. It was. When his dad came out of the hospital, Country let go of my hand, ran full speed to his dad, and yelled, "Daddy!" I can't imagine the healing that came with that first hug that they both needed so much.

I moved to East Texas so my son could get to know his dad and their family. The whole time I held onto my grandmother's last plea to put our families back together. I didn't know how I would repair the past, but I gave it my best effort. It was hard being in Palestine again, especially without my grandmother. I struggled. I reconnected with my childhood sweetheart, my first boyfriend ever, the guy who had wanted to marry me when I was fourteen years old. We kicked off a whirlwind relationship that led to a wedding six weeks later. With every ounce of my misguided heart, I thought I was doing what God wanted me to do. I didn't stop to think things through, I just decided and acted on it. I had inaccurate information about the state of his mental health and his addiction recovery timeline, and I didn't allow enough time for the truth to surface.

BOND with me on this hard lesson. God doesn't rush timing. When we feel rushed to make decisions in emotional urgency, it's usually an "us thing," and not a "God thing." While getting married felt like all of the pieces of my life were falling into place, I was ignoring the red flags that were waving at me because I honestly didn't want to see them. Here was this guy, who had loved me and wanted to marry me since I was fourteen, and it all seemed like the best option for our future. I conceded that nobody had ever loved me like he had.

The marriage was rough, pretty much from the beginning. At first I didn't understand the drastic mood swings. The good times were great, and the bad times were really scary. I remember the first time he called me a derogatory name, I was taken aback. Nobody had ever talked to me like that. He had emptied his pockets onto the bed, which were filled with loose change and little bolts and washers he'd picked up throughout the day while working as a mechanic. About the third time he called me that name, I put my six years of childhood softball success and being a third generation pitcher to good use and started throwing those greasy coins and things at him. He left the room, and I heard him digging through the kitchen drawers. I grew extremely fearful that he was looking for a knife. I hid.

Within a few months, he went through his first binge, and that's when I discovered that I was married to a drug addict. I had never even experimented with drugs, so I had no idea how to relate to his battle. We fought constantly, but I wanted a family more than anything, so I didn't take a stand. I thought I could love him through it, and that he'd have an incredible testimony of God saving him from addiction. But, to make matters worse, he stopped taking the medication that helped him with Bipolar Disorder, and his mood swings grew even scarier.

I thought I could be supportive enough to help him see his strengths and talents. I looked at him, not as the person he was, but as the person I knew God intended him to be. I didn't presume I could change him, but I believed God could. I clung to the hope that God would. I made so many mistakes. Once again, I was not a very good wife. I was a terrible housekeeper, I had minimal cooking skills, and I wasn't very good at bringing peace to our home. I still didn't have healthy boundaries. I held onto a marriage that was destroying me because I didn't want to be a two-time divorcee. I tried to force things I shouldn't have...like having a baby early.

I knew in my heart that having a baby would not fix my marital problems, but I did believe that it would make me happy. Being a mom was the best part of my life. When those two blue lines appeared on the pregnancy test not long after we married, I was elated. It was no surprise to our family and friends that an early pregnancy didn't smooth out my relationship with my husband. Finances were tight, emotions ran hot, and it felt like we fought all the time.

My entire mental health changed dramatically in one horrific tragedy on December 10, 2006. The beginning of my anxiety, panic attacks, and self-harm can all be traced back to that day. Most people who self-harm start in their teenage years, but I didn't begin cutting myself until I lost my son, Caden Samuel, almost 20 weeks into my pregnancy. The devastating pain I experienced from that loss was greater than any other I had ever felt. A part of me shut down, and I adopted coping mechanisms; most were destructive.

During the week of Thanksgiving, on Tuesday, November 21st, I sat at the doctor's office alone for a routine checkup, hoping to schedule my sonogram for the next week that would reveal whether I was having a boy or girl. I was convinced that I was having a girl and that her name would be Hannah, because I had dreamed it. After a series of tests, the doctor told me as gently as possible, that I was going to lose the baby. They couldn't hear the heartbeat. They wanted to induce labor and end the pregnancy. I wasn't as heartbroken as I was fiercely determined that they didn't understand God's power. "No. You're wrong. This baby will be a miracle, you watch." I believed it with every ounce of my faith. I left against medical advice and called every prayer warrior we knew. I never told anyone all that was said, just that we needed a miracle, and I put my whole heart on the line to believe that I would have a miracle baby. With every day that passed, I believed more. I rubbed my growing tummy while I sang to him, rocking slowly each night. I prayed over him and talked to him. If wanting that child could have made it all okay, he'd be here now. When I started bleeding on December 10, I knew it was over, and I lost a part of myself when I lost that pregnancy.

It was in that darkness where I sought ways to express a deep-rooted grief that tormented me. I walked around feeling like a zombie going through the motions of life. I questioned my faith more than anything. I didn't understand how God could take him. I didn't understand what was wrong with my faith that I couldn't believe strong enough to have a miracle. I believed that I was the problem. I questioned why I had dreamed I was having a girl named Hannah, when the baby had actually been a boy. Later, much later, God showed me that the baby wasn't Hannah, but that I was. He *had* heard my cries for a baby, and though I couldn't see it at the time, God knew exactly what He was doing.

My journey to healing after Caden took a long time, and it still stings to this day. Thankfully, I had excellent support through our church and the pastors, David and Susan Haines. They were the ones who encouraged me to name the baby. "You have to stop talking about him like he wasn't here. He will always be a part of you. Name him," Susan encouraged me gently. At home, by myself, through the endless tears of a broken heart, I named Caden Samuel and let God take the hurt away just a little bit. There was healing in acknowledging him and accepting that he would always be a part of me, and that I didn't have to hang on to the pain to keep him with me. I could focus on the times I felt him kick, and heard his heartbeat, and sung to him. I could dream of what his life would have been like on this earth and what it would be like to hold him again in heaven. I could step forward in life and bring him with me. I had to understand that I didn't owe it to him to stay stuck in grief. Tragedy was not the currency for my peace. It hurt to step forward and broke my heart beyond belief.

The marriage never recovered; we stayed together for five years. Not only was I under the stress of an emotionally unstable relationship, grieving Caden, and extreme financial duress, but at the end of the relationship, I was working two full-time jobs and taking seventeen hours of college courses. My ex-husband's drug addiction was a steady stressor. A couple of years into our marriage, I started getting debilitating migraines and seizures. The doctor said that my physical body couldn't hold up to the mental and emotional pressure I was under. It was slowly killing me.

The doctor took my mom aside to explain the importance of slowing me down. I was physically, emotionally, mentally, and even spiritually stretched beyond my limits. I had to make changes. However, I convinced myself that because of the migraines, I couldn't take care of myself. For months at a time, my husband would take care of me. He'd stay sober for a few months, and then he'd binge for a few days. During that time, I internalized his struggle. In my mind, his addiction meant I wasn't enough for him. I viewed it as abandonment and rejection that he chose drugs over me.

The pain that tethered itself to my identity was abandonment. There was a time I had a flat tire on the side of the road. I couldn't reach him because he was getting high with his friends. Another time, I was being released from a hospital stay and had to find a ride home because he didn't come pick me up. The biggest scare came when I was selling merchandise at a flea market. We had set up my table in a large parking lot near the highway and had a good show. He spent the day there with me. As the event began to wind down, we planned that he would pick up my son, and they would return to help me load everything up. When he left, he took most of the money from our sales and left in our only car. The trip should have only taken an hour, but he stopped and got drugs along the way, never picked up my son, and didn't come back to get me. I was stuck on the side of the road with my table, my merchandise, very little cash, and no phone. I was ten miles from home and had no way to get there or get to my son.

There were times he left me stranded at work. Bank accounts were repeatedly emptied, or he would sell our things for cash. Every time he left, I felt more and more worthless. By the time I got the courage to say "never again," it wasn't because I believed that I was worth it, but because I wanted to protect my son from further pain.

I vowed that I would never again allow myself to need people or depend on them. But as with most declarations made out of self-preservation, I just wanted to protect myself from pain. I didn't feel worthy of love because I was the kind of girl who got left on the side of the road. *That* was the truth I accepted. My entire evaluation of my self-worth was tied up in one moment of one day: I was the kind of girl that you just forget.

BOND with me here. How I allowed him to treat me became tied to my identity. It literally became part of how I saw myself. His choices and actions became enmeshed with my identity, because I didn't empower myself to stand up and say that I was worth more. Before I could change the way I was treated, I had to deconstruct and rebuild the way I valued myself.

CHAPTER THIRTEEN

The Right to Say No

In the summer of 2011, a few months after my second divorce, I met Coach at a sports camp my son attended. We hit it off immediately, but I had learned my lesson from the first divorce and did not rush into another relationship. I wasn't ready to date, but we had discussed the option. We flirted a lot. We even had some conversations that went way too far sexually. We talked almost every day about life and saw each other occasionally. Country, eleven at the time, thought Coach was the absolute coolest guy ever. I could see myself with him long-term, but then life fell apart again.

In September, I drove myself to the hospital in the middle of the night in terrible pain. I had an ovarian cyst that had ruptured, and they couldn't give me pain medicine without someone else present to drive me home. It was late, and I didn't know who to call, so I called Coach. He came and sat by my side while I alternated between throwing up and crying. He was a trooper, totally there for me through it all. Even when they told me that they found a mass on my ovary, and it didn't look good, he was right there.

A couple of days later, on September 3rd, I sat in the doctor's office and listened as he explained that I needed an emergency hysterectomy. My cycles were nine days apart, I had miscarried five times, I was getting softball sized cysts, and there was a mass that needed to be removed. To make it even scarier, the cancer markers in my bloodwork indicated that I was about to embark on the battle of my life. The doctor prepared me that I'd probably be starting chemo right after surgery, and that an oncologist would visit me in the hospital after the biopsies. I was 32 years old and beyond devastated to give up hope of having more biological children.

After surgery, the doctor sat in my room and told me that he couldn't explain what he saw or how different it was from the tests before surgery. While there had a been a large mass in my uterus, and they were confident that it was the cause of the miscarriages, they didn't see the number of cancerous cells they expected. They removed the only cancer cells present, so I didn't have to have chemotherapy after all. Recovery went well until October 31, 2011.

I had gone to the doctor in Dallas and was on a mission to get released back to work quickly. However, once at the doctor's office, I just didn't feel right. I can't really describe it much better than that. It was like a really bad migraine, but worse. Something just felt off. I kept thinking that if I could just get home and rest, I'd be fine. But as I drove home, the symptoms got worse. I was going down Highway 175 and saw the exit for the hospital in Kaufman. I caught a glimpse of myself in the mirror and the whole left side of my face was drooping. I had my hands laced together at the top of the steering wheel while leaning forward, a position I often drove in when I couldn't get comfortable. When I began to turn the car toward the left exit that would take me to the hospital, my left arm just fell from the wheel, and I couldn't pick it back up.

I managed to pull into the parking lot of the hospital and drug myself into the ER, looking very much like Quasimodo in three-inch heels. As I came through the glass doors, the receptionist caught sight of my dangling arm, dragging left leg, and drooping face, and jumped over the reception desk screaming for a wheelchair. With my blood pressure at 195/114 and the left-side paralysis, I was quickly diagnosed with a stroke and CareFlited to Dallas Presbyterian.

After a week in ICU and every stroke test known to man, they finally figured out that I had not had a stroke, but rather an extremely rare migraine disorder called Hemiplegic Migraines. These rare migraines cause the vessels in the brain to constrict, resulting in stroke-like symptoms. The migraines can last for hours, days, weeks, or even months. That migraine lasted 96 days and almost cost me my life. I was faced with hundreds of unanswered questions because the disease is so rare, and few doctors knew how to treat it.

At one off my specialist appointments with a man I only refer to as "Dr. Jerk," he walked into the room, sat at a table, and flatly asked, "What do you want from me?"

I was over two months into a migraine, so I didn't respond in kindness. I retorted, "For you not to be a jerk."

He wasn't fazed, "What do you want?"

I pushed back tears, defeated, and I said, "For you to help me."

He looked straight at me and without even blinking, he said, "Nobody can help you. You're going to have a stroke, and you're going to die."

Just like that. No emotion, nothing. He urged me to go to the Mayo Clinic where they had some experimental protocols, but told me that every migraine could be my next stroke and the prognosis was day-to-day.

My life was in complete chaos. Meanwhile, I was battling my identity as a single woman, twice divorced. I was trying to move forward with my life and pick up the pieces of my new normal. On December 7th I invited Coach over to my house for the first time. We hadn't talked as much during my recovery but had starting texting more in the weeks leading up to him coming over. He agreed to join my son and I for dinner around 7 PM. I made dinner, got ready, but dinner time came and went. No Coach. I fed my son, and we watched a movie. He went to bed around 10 PM with lots of questions about why Coach had not come over. At 11 PM, there was a knock on my door. It was Coach. I let him in, but I was mad at him for blowing off dinner.

We talked, and like I always did back then, I quickly caved. Talking became kissing, and kissing became a heavy make out session. Then things went wrong. Coach became overly aggressive. When I wanted to stop, he didn't. Less than three months out from a having a full hysterectomy, I was still sore. When I told him he was hurting me, he told me to "lay back and take it."

I instantly went into that dark place of childhood abuse. I stopped fighting, silenced my cries, and committed to survive the storm of pain. Tears streamed down my face the whole time, but he never looked at me. When he was satisfied, he collapsed on top of me, told me not to move, and went to sleep. More tears came, but I refused to make a sound. I didn't want my son to hear or come into the room.

I didn't know how to classify what had happened. We'd had numerous sexual conversations, and we had made out consensually that night. I felt like I had invited trouble. I settled on calling it a "date gone wrong" and tried to move on. People around me knew there was something different about me. I began to withdraw from everyone I knew and loved. I had bags under my eyes because I couldn't sleep at night. I was irritable and jumpy. I replayed the scene over and over in my head, telling myself that I deserved it because I invited him to my house. He wasn't just some random guy.

It took a lot of counseling to recover from that night and to stop reliving it in my sleep. I was suffering from shock and shame. I couldn't reconcile his actions with who he was, one of my closest friends. He became someone I didn't recognize. I would later have the opportunity to confront him. I am glad I did, but it was one of the most difficult conversations I've ever had. Eventually, I accepted the fact that it was a terrible night, that he wasn't who I thought he was, and it should have never happened. I stopped blaming myself and somewhere down the road in my healing journey, I would discover that no matter what, I had the right to say no.

CHAPTER FOURTEEN

False Sense of Security

"I hate the scale. I hate cameras. I hate my body." Those were the most frequent phrases I wrote in my journal for years. My lifelong battle with weight began when I was 12 years old and I had made a conscious decision to gain weight because I equated being heavy to safety. In addition to non-existent physical boundaries, my biological father also lacked boundaries in communication and often shared inappropriate information with me. After hearing the graphic and negative comments he made about obese women, I came up with a plan to gain weight so that I would never be abused again. In my twelve-year-old mind, it made total sense.

I remained chubby until I started dating my first boyfriend. I wasn't morbidly obese, but I kept enough weight on me to feel safe. At some point it became an unconscious connotation between the extra pounds and safety. However, as a young adult I became obsessed with weight loss. Working at the gentleman's club had triggered body insecurities for me. I began skipping meals and eventually stopped eating all together. The more weight I lost, the more people complimented me, and the higher tips I received as a waitress. That was the beginning of anorexia for me.

I began to train my body to go without food for days at a time. It started off with just skipping one day of food, then two, then a week...then two weeks. The day I found I was pregnant with my son, I hadn't eaten in twenty-three days. I was literally slowly killing myself. I had a choice to make. The doctor was going to hospitalize me and force me to eat for the sake of my pregnancy, or I could fix the problem and report back to the doctor every week for a weigh-in. I determined that I could and would fix the problem. I vowed to never starve myself again, and I didn't. However, without healthy boundaries, I quickly turned to eating whatever I wanted, whenever I wanted. I gained sixty-five pounds when I was pregnant, and I didn't lose it. Over the years, I added on 5-10 pounds every year, and found myself over 300 pounds in 2011 at the end of my marriage.

I had lap band surgery in 2011 and was very successful in keeping my weight down for the first nine months. I lost 110 pounds and went from size 24 to size 12 while going through a divorce. It was not my goal weight, but I was smaller than I had been since I got pregnant with my son. When I started getting debilitating migraines, my weight loss continued, but not in a healthy way. That worsened in September when I had to have the hysterectomy, and the doctors took all the fluid out of my lap band. I made poor food choices and ate almost anything I wanted again. Without an exercise plan or healthy diet, I regained eighty pounds that I had lost. I went through phases where I'd start a diet and lose 20-30 pounds and then give up and regain it all, plus five more.

As an adult, I didn't notice my pattern of weight gain after a heart break. I would date some new, and when it would go south, I'd gain weight. That pattern continued throughout the next seven years, and in 2018, after taking my son to the Mayo Clinic for a medical diagnosis, I got a reality check about my health and determined that I needed to make healthier life choices. I started working out. A friend saw a workout post that I put on Facebook and invited me to Camp Gladiator.

Camp Gladiator is an hour-long bootcamp style workout completed outdoors in a group format. The comradery is highly motivating, and I quickly became obsessed with it. While it is not recommended to do more than three CG workouts per week because it is hard on your joints, I was hooked. I went every day. The more results I saw, the more frequently I went. Then there were days that I went twice. A few days, I even did three workouts!

The results were unlike anything I had ever seen in my life. I was on a dangerously low-carb diet, eating fewer than 15g of carbohydrates a day. I did fifty workouts and lost fifty pounds in fifty days. That kind of progress only pushed me harder. I lost a total of one hundred pounds and did one hundred workouts in one hundred and twenty days. I felt like a new person. However, my knees hurt excruciatingly, and I started a job working two hours away from home. I got out of the habit of going to workouts. As I reintroduced carbohydrates into my diet, I started gaining the weight back rapidly. In April 2019, I had to have an emergency procedure to remove my lap band. In May, my grandfather had a stroke, and in July, he passed away.

All of that compounded when I had my heart completely shattered by a guy who had been in my life for more than fifteen years. I was struggling, and the whole time I was struggling, I gained weight. When I found myself once again defeated and back at the beginning of my weight loss journey, I did some serious soul searching. That was when I remembered gaining weight on purpose when I was twelve. I also recalled how many times I had gained weight when I had been hurt, specifically when I was hurt by men. Instead of confronting and processing my pain, I retreated behind a giant wall of food. I became overweight again and counted on people not to see past my exterior or want to get close to my heart. I ate until I felt safe.

I had to confront the root cause of my weight problem. I needed to acknowledge and address that I used my weight as a security blanket. After I started trusting God to keep me safe, I saw improvements in my weight battle. I stopped binge eating and gained control over my portions. I stopped pushing aside emotions and turning to food. I stopped fad dieting and obsessing over workouts. I am not where I want to be in my health journey, but for the first time in my life, I am losing weight *because* I am making healthy decisions instead of making healthy decisions *just to* lose the weight.

As part of my daily reading routine, I read a chapter in Proverbs every day. Proverbs introduced me to God as a Father. Throughout the book of Proverbs, numerous scriptures tell about wisdom and guidance and how they protect us. It reads like a book of letters from a loving parent, telling their child everything they would want them to know if they weren't going to be around to say it. As I read Proverbs, I read God's letters to me, instructing me how to live my life, how to fix my mess, and where to focus my efforts in order to achieve success. Previously, I found ways to protect myself which were indulgent and unhealthy. But when I found scriptures, like the ones in Proverbs 3 that explain that wisdom, knowledge, common sense, and discernment are the tools God gave me to protect myself from calamity (not food), I found healthy ways to manage pain, stress, and heartache.

CHAPTER FIFTEEN

Purpose in Poverty

I never finished college, so I couldn't become a classroom teacher like I wanted to for many years. The only roles I qualified to fill in education were paraprofessional roles. That meant that I worked full-time, earning less than $20,000 a year. I dreamed of being a classroom teacher but found every reason to quit college while juggling mom duties and working multiple jobs. There came a time during the 2016-2017 school year, toward the end of the first semester, that the weight of working multiple jobs seemed heavier than I could bear. Even with multiple streams of income, we were far below the poverty line. My son was a freshman, and I knew that I couldn't afford college for him on what I made. It took every ounce of strength and courage I could muster to turn in my notice at the school and accept a short contract role doing IT support.

No matter how hard I worked, or how successful I became, it didn't change one undeniable fact: I missed my kids at school. We stayed in touch for a long time, and they understood that I had to take care of my family, but they had been devasted when I left, and I carried that guilt with me daily. The leadership group I had led was a close-knit family that went on camps together, came to my house, hung out together, did community events, and truly made a difference in the community. We grew from fourteen student leaders to more than 200 in six months. It was one of the coolest projects I have ever been a part of.

I look back in amazement that something so powerful literally came out of a dream. At two o'clock in the morning, I sat up and grabbed a pen and paper to write out the project plan before I forgot anything I had seen. Named after our school's behavior acronyms, The P.R.I.D.E. Project (Purpose, Respect, Integrity, Dedication, Expectation) was my life's work. I wanted to do that job every day for the rest of my life. It was intrinsically rewarding, so I justified having to pick up multiple side jobs to keep the lights on because I was making a difference, and it felt good.

I never intended to do technical support long-term. I considered several career paths such as Cyber Security and computer programming, where I knew I could achieve my financial goals quickly. As a helpdesk analyst, my income was just enough to replace the three jobs I had worked previously, but it still didn't stretch very far. I was making right at $35,000 a year and commuting 60 miles one way to do it. My income wasn't below the poverty line anymore, but it wasn't soaring too far above it either.

I discovered something important about myself while working the IT position. If I don't relate to a problem that someone is sharing with me, I am not quite as empathetic as I should be. That discovery came while I was on the phone with a gentleman who was panicked over a computer problem, he deemed serious. During the call I realized that I didn't want to work all day helping people fix their computers—mostly because I refuse to believe you are having an actual Excel spreadsheet crisis. I was making more money, and my hour-long commute gave me plenty to write about in *Andi On a Train*, a fun blog about being a complete anxiety-stricken germaphobe riding public transportation.

My helpdesk contract came to a pretty abrupt end when I was hospitalized for a severe infection caused by a large kidney stone. I spent nine days in the hospital and had two surgeries during that time. The company I worked for would only hold my job for three days. As a contractor, the company could end my contract at any time for any reason; FMLA did not apply to me. Fortunately for me, the recruiter who got me the job saw something in me that made her think I'd make a great recruiter. During my final five days in the hospital, I applied for over two hundred entry-level recruiting jobs online. I finally found a foot in the door of a recruiting agency and began a career that would eventually change my financial trajectory.

Recruiting just made sense to me. It was simple math. Either you knew the person and their skills, and you were finding them a job, or you knew the job and the skills, and you were finding the person. It was as simple as solving for x. I was goal driven, and every time I broke a company record, I became more focused on my goal of making six figures. I worked nonstop. It was not uncommon for me to start my day at 4 AM and end it at 11 PM. However, I was used to hard work. I worked 50-60 hours a week at the school and multiple other jobs, so working one job 80-90 hours per week didn't really faze me.

When I began recruiting, I decided that I would work one job with the same hours and effort that I had previously worked two jobs. I had three years left before Country went to college, which meant that my time had to result in maximum financial impact. I was on a self-appointed mission to show my son once and for all what success looked like. At that time in my life, I viewed success as a destination. I fantasized success as somewhere you arrive after a hard-work-induced torrent of blood, sweat, and tears. I didn't know anything about my final destination except that I thought it needed a six-figure income attached to it. That was my end goal: make six figures while working a job that felt important to me, gave me a sense of purpose, and made a difference in the lives of others. I was determined to get to that imaginary place and then show my son the way. I would say things like, "The only thing that stands in between you and your dream is hard work." I had no idea that I was projecting my workaholic lifestyle onto my son. Had I not eventually realized what I was doing to him and stopped it, I would have perpetuated a generational cycle of addiction.

My dream wasn't overly complicated, and my intentions were good. I wanted to be able to pay all of my bills in the same month. That's it. That's all I wanted. My vision board wasn't shiny or flashy. It was the wall of bills staring me down every day and taunting me at night. Another bill would come in, and I'd tack it to the wall, adding it to the other past due notices. They weighed on my heart and mind constantly as I juggled which bills to pay to avoid eviction and keep the utilities on. I had turned all of my focus toward changing my financial situation because I struggled with daily guilt for raising my son in poverty his whole life. Every time we had to move because of an eviction, or that I went outside and found my car had been repossessed, I always promised to figure it out, even when I had no idea how I would.

I constantly juggled the utilities being on and off. There were quite a few sweltering nights in the Texas summer heat when we moved around a dark house by candlelight or flashlight and then tossed and turned miserably all night because it was so hot that we stuck to the sheets. There were even a few times when I loaded my son in the car in the early morning hours and took him to the school where I worked, even before the janitors arrived, so each of us could shower in the nurse's office because we didn't have water at home. Every time I fed him Ramen Noodles or a dollar can of Chef Boyardee Ravioli for dinner, or each time I made one pot of chili to last all week crushed me, and I was even more compelled to work longer hours. Every commission check drove me to work harder because I saw the fruits of my labor and felt like my efforts were beginning to pay off.

However, as is common with entry level jobs, the first one was terrible. There was yelling and screaming; there was cattiness and drama; there was banging on desks; and there was backstabbing. Being in a toxic culture, working long hours, trying to build a business, and still trying to be super-mom took its toll. It didn't take long for the panic attacks to gain momentum to the point where they were happening almost daily.

CHAPTER SIXTEEN

Fight, Flight, or Freeze

One night, I was driving home from work when the all too familiar symptoms suddenly struck. I couldn't catch my breath, my heart pounded, and my chest hurt. I felt dizzy as the overwhelming sense of panic closed in on me. I navigated my car to the side of the road and turned on my emergency flashers. I listened to the constant click on and off of the emergency indicators that told other drivers passing by that I was in a state of distress. I tried to slow my breathing while I mentally chastised myself that it was "all in my head." I picked up the phone and called a friend. I just wanted someone to talk to me, about anything, just to get my mind off of the horrible claustrophobic feeling of not being able to breath. They didn't answer.

I tried my mom and my sister. Voicemails. It was late, and I called nine different people, but none of them answered. I was alone...very, very alone. While the walls in my car seemed to close in on all sides, I cracked the window just a bit, trying to get fresh air. I sat in my dark car on the side of the road in complete silence except for tattered breathing and the annoyingly steady rhythm of those stupid emergency flashing lights that ticked along with the demand in my brain, "breathe, breathe, breathe, breathe..."

I thought about all the times my friends had tried to reach out to me, but I had been working. Eventually they had stopped calling. The missed baby showers, wedding showers, and girls' nights added up. I had isolated myself completely. With each negative thought, the walls closed in tighter. Depression and anxiety swirled around inside my head. I was convinced I was going to die in my car on the side of the Chisolm Trail Toll Road.

In that moment, something on the inside of me whispered, "Hold your breath." The thought was so foreign, but I had nothing to lose, so I decided to listen to my inner voice and give it a shot. I stopped fighting against the hyperventilation, gulped as much air as I possibly could and held my breath. I didn't know how long I was going to hold my breath, and I really didn't know why I was doing it. I just started counting the seconds one by one as my mind raced. After twenty seconds, I began to feel my lungs tighten. By thirty seconds, my heart rate quickened. By forty seconds, my eyes began to water. My brain was screaming in sync with my emergency flashers, "Breathe...breathe...breathe..." At forty -six seconds, I gasped for air. Breathe.

For a few seconds after exhaling, I panted while taking unnaturally deep breaths. As my breathing evened out and my heart rate slowed, I realized that I wasn't panicked anymore. I was pretty confused about what just happened. My heart rate slowly returned to normal, my thoughts cleared, holding my breath worked, and I had no idea why. Once my mind was clear, I drove myself home, with my mind focused on "what just happened?" As any overthinker would do, I set out to analyze the exact order of events, and then began a life-changing research project about anxiety and panic attacks.

The first thing I realized was that while I was holding my breath, I focused solely on counting the seconds which broke the mental trap that a panic attack creates. Instead of my brain having free reign to hyperfocus on the symptoms of the attack, I had put myself in charge of the reactions my body was having. My brain was no longer triaging the reason why I couldn't breathe, by holding my breath I was solely responsible for the symptoms my body was experiencing. I understood what I was feeling and why I was feeling that way. More importantly, I understood how to fix it. I was the one holding my breath and withholding oxygen from myself. If I wanted to breathe, all I had to do was inhale and exhale like I had been doing my whole life. I had successfully found my own Jedi mind trick that took my brain out of panic mode and set me back in control of my thoughts.

I have never had a medical professional explain what was happening in my body when I was having a panic attack, even when I was being treated for anxiety. For me, I felt more equipped in my battle against anxiety when I knew what was happening in my body. I learned a few important things while doing online medical research— not Googling my medical symptoms because 90% of the research led to incurable diseases or cancer, which I didn't have. *Somehow leading people who already have anxiety to a panic-inducing article on terrifying diseases seems cruel.* Out of self-preservation I found more resourceful and less scary results by adding words like, "fighting," "overcoming," and "coping with" in front of my search words. For example, the articles were much more valuable to me when I searched "overcoming anxiety," rather than just searching "panic attacks."

When I started the research project, I was actually on a mission to find out whether I was completely crazy or not. Surely if controlling anxiety was a simple as holding your breath, I would not have been the first person to discover that, and it turned out, I wasn't. It's a real thing. The practice is much more common in the UK and is somewhat controversial among doctors, but many physicians endorse the practice within healthy limitations.

I learned that the feeling of shortness of breath was not that my body was deprived of oxygen. There wasn't a problem with my respiratory system itself. My lungs were fine, and my airways were clear. While under perceived stress, I was taking in less air than I was forcing out. Similar to how I would hyperventilate for a few moments after being startled. When my body forced the carbon monoxide out of my lungs too quickly, it triggered the amygdala (which is the emotional processing center) in my brain to initiate the fight, flight, or freeze response that it was designed to do. Essentially, I concluded that we are all designed to respond naturally to panic based on the perception of a threat. The reaction we experience depends upon our brain's perception of how well we can handle the perceived threat. The key word repeated over and over in this research was *perception*. In crisis mode, my brain responded to perception, not to facts.

I was captivated by the research and dove deeper to explore the concepts behind fight, flight, or freeze. Before that project, I actually didn't even know about the freeze option. I had paid minimal attention in a few college Psych classes, enough to pass tests and earn credit for the class, but not enough to gain a full understanding of some core concepts. Basically, I simplified fight and flight as mutually exclusive. I thought everyone could be classified as either a fighter or a runner. I accepted that I was wired for flight since I perceived that as my go-to reaction. I was shocked to learn that none of us are actually wired completely for one response. It totally depends on the threat we face and how we perceive the threat in relation to ourselves.

If my brain perceives that I have a fair chance to conquer a battle, then my response will be to fight. The fight response kicks in when I feel like, "Okay, I got this." The fight response is my favorite, mostly because of the total fierce warrior connotation with the word *fight*. When I hear about a fight response, I think of strength and feistiness. I picture someone completely unstoppable and totally fearless. However, there is more to the fight response than that, like when someone has given me fearless feedback, and I completely and totally claws-out lash out.

The fight response triggered in me when I perceived someone as a threat to my comfort zone. So, I'd fight to keep them out of the spaces of my heart that hurt most. Sometimes I would fight really hard to keep people out who were actually supposed to be in my life. I found that the fight response, when fueled by strength and determination, enabled me to achieve goals that were far beyond my reach. However, when the fight response was induced by fear or insecurity, it usually resulted in heartache.

I associate my fight response to the way I confronted the ninety-six-day migraine, earning my own hashtag. *#CowgirlTuff is still my favorite hashtag in the history of ever*. I didn't start out ready to fight, it wasn't until Dr. Nissan provided hope for a medical breakthrough that I gloved up ready to rally. My support team gathered around me, and we fought. Maybe the most important lesson I learned while discovering my inner Laila Ali, was that I could trigger a warrior response to fight back even if I didn't believe in my own ability to handle a situation, but I fully believed in God's.

Throughout my life, I have been more of a flight kind of girl. I never ran very well in a physical sense. Okay, that's not true, I never ran *at all* in a physical sense, but emotionally, I was quite the triathlete. In my research, I learned that the flight response was triggered by my view of a problem or situation that I perceived as bigger and stronger than me, but that I also believed I had an adequate escape route from. When I faced a big problem that I perceived I could outrun, I did some record-breaking, Forrest Gump kind of emotional running.

Running showed itself in various forms. It could be as simple as changing the subject mid-conversation, the art of which I mastered beautifully, I must say. The flight response made me hang up on bill collectors and telemarketers. *I'm okay with that one.* Since our brains are wired to avoid pain, another flight tactic I fully embraced was procrastination. When faced with a dreaded task, my flight response kicked in, and it simply became another checkbox on the to-do list that haunted me at night.

Sometimes fleeing carried with it much greater consequences than simply steering a conversation to a more comfortable place. I often quit things I started. I frequently ran as far and as fast as I could away from good people. Still, no matter how hard I sprinted from my problems, eventually they caught up with me. There would come a time when I would have to face challenges head on and find the courage to fight. Flight exhibited itself in various ways as well, like when I got defensive and lied to my son's father about Country being his, then ran back home to my parents' house. It was flight that kicked in when I left houses in the middle of the night to avoid the eviction process. Sometimes surviving meant getting out of the way before an explosion.

I had to reexamine my self-identify and change some limiting self-beliefs before I could accept that I was actually worth fighting for. I was definitely worth the effort it took to learn to fight for myself. There was an awakening in my spirit when I finally acknowledged that fighting for what I wanted or what I believed in was not clingy, needy, or demanding.

There is a third option in response to crisis: it's to freeze. This is where the panic attacks came into play for me. When I was faced with a problem that I knew was bigger, stronger, tougher, and faster than me, and there was absolutely no way I could beat it or get away from it, I would freeze. It really didn't matter in the moment what the problem was, but rather how I perceived it in relation to my worth and abilities. For example, I often froze when going to an event where there would be people I didn't know. It was pretty common for me to go somewhere and then text from the parking lot that something came up and I couldn't make it to the event, never telling anyone that I actually drove there, but had a full panic attack in my car. Asking for a special order at a restaurant or sending food back if it came out incorrectly was rarely worth the embarrassment for me. I would try to muster the courage to bring it to the server's attention but would usually freeze up in a panic and simply ask for a refill on my drink.

My panic attacks usually started with some version of the thought "I can't do this." As I responded to crises in my life, there came a point when my mind no longer trusted my ability to process the information or deal with the problem, resulting in a panic attack. Some frequent triggers included extreme financial duress, work conflicts, family conflicts, break ups, looming deadlines, or when I had taken on too many projects and felt completely overloaded. I didn't have good boundaries and often put myself up against unnecessary deadlines or took on projects I shouldn't have.

During panic attacks, I didn't treat myself with the same grace or kindness that I would have extended to others in the same situation. Often, my self-talk sounded like: *Andi, just stop. You're being ridiculous. This is all in your head. You don't have time for crazy right now. Get it together!* Those words only served to exacerbate the panic attack. Negative self-talk perpetuated my feelings of inadequacy and ate away at my ability to handle the situation. However, the situation wasn't going to change or just go away because I refused to deal with it. Unfortunately, life doesn't always provide the "no thank you, I don't want to do this" option. However, I could change *my perception* of my ability to deal with the situation.

Equipped with better strategies, I am able to deal with panic attacks more effectively now. When a panic attack strikes, I take a deep breath in through my nose while paying close attention to the feeling of my lungs filling up with air just as they were designed to do. I start my affirmation by thinking to myself, *My body is functioning properly. I was designed to breath and to fight for life. My life is worth fighting for.* I exhale very slowly while centering my thoughts again, *I am in control of my body's responses. I am safe. I can handle this situation.* I take another breath and think, *I have the mind of Christ. I am at peace. I am safe.* I exhale sharply through my mouth. On the third inhale, I hold my breath again and think, *Just as God breathed life into Adam's nostrils, I was created to breathe. Just breathe.* After the last exhale, I note one action step I can do to begin moving forward. For example, when entering a room of new people my action step is to immediately turn and introduce myself to someone new.

Much like training at the gym, there were times that it hurt to train my mind, but I was determined to keep going. There were times that I wanted to quit trying and just stay a mess because my comfort zone was a dot far off in the distance. I kept digging deeper. For me, anxiety was the surface problem. Depression and a broken self-image were the underliers.

Okay, BOND with me for a second. Do any of these phrases sound familiar? "You don't know how I feel," "You don't know what happened," "You just don't understand," or what about, "You don't know what I've been through." Those slogans are scrawled out in Sharpie on the posters I hold in the emotional picket lines in my heart. As a survivor of tragedy and trauma, I carried my past around with me everywhere I went. I was like an adult girl scout with a vest that boasted scars as badges of honor. I was ready to point to any one of them when I needed to justify why I was acting or responding in a particular way. I stopped doing that once I learned that in the moment just before I pushed someone out of my emotional space with a heart-felt, "You don't know how far I've come," my fight, flight, or freeze response was triggered.

If someone I cared about or respected broached a tough topic, I had a tendency to freeze. The perceived threat for me was the risk of disappointing them or losing their friendship if I said the wrong thing. However, if the person giving me feedback was someone I felt like I could step away from without any long-term consequences, I ran. If a stranger, or someone who had no real voice in my life tried to say something hurtful or threatening, I fought.

I had a brick wall I could throw up any time someone hedged too close to a trigger topic. Something as simple a word or phrase that evoked a negative memory, could cause me to lash out in anger, even if it was intended as a joke. Mid-journey there was no room for jokes about topics I deemed off limits. The biggest problem was that others didn't know my trigger topics, and they we blindsided when I responded with venom.

I'd throw up a wall when someone tried to give me constructive criticism because in my head all I heard was, "You aren't good enough." I grew defensive because I saw my efforts, while they only saw my results. I rejected some really great advice because I wasn't ready to hear it. I would flee a situation because of my insecurity that I was *not enough.* When people gave me fearless feedback, I wasn't rude to them, *usually,* but inside I was thinking, *You don't know what's it's cost me to be here. You don't know how far I've come.*

In truth, it wasn't where I had been that was destroying me. It wasn't childhood abuse that broke me. It wasn't the loss of loved ones or teenage depression. It wasn't the first failed marriage...or even the second. It wasn't having my first child at nineteen or raising him alone. It wasn't five miscarriages that shattered me, though they certainly threatened to. I was still standing after the date gone wrong. When I had to have a full hysterectomy—burying my hopes of ever having another biological child—it was a setback in my faith, but I did survive. Even when I was diagnosed with a rare migraine disorder that caused horrific pain and endangered my life for months, I was not destroyed. All of those experiences were beyond challenging, they were horrific. But none of them—singularly, nor collectively—broke me.

What shattered my heart was when I stopped being the person that God called me to be and stopped doing the things that God called me to do. I could not find peace in my life until I was at peace with my lifestyle and my life choices.

God showed me something beautiful about the battle going on in my mind that surpassed anxiety and encompassed my struggles with mental and emotional bondage. Sitting in the car that fateful day, holding my breath, when my mind asked the question, "Do I even want to live?" my body answered with a resounding *YES!* Yes, when deprived of air, my body fought to do exactly what it was designed to do—live. I was designed to breathe. My body was made to live and fight for life. As I held my breath and carbon monoxide built up in my lungs, it became painful. My diaphragm kicked in like internal CPR and spasmed to trigger involuntary reflexes designed to make me breathe again. As I continued to deprive myself of oxygen, the spasms increased, becoming more painful. My brain was screaming, "Just breathe!" Finally, I couldn't fight it anymore, and I sucked in a gasp of air.

During those forty-six seconds of holding my breath, my body just did what it was designed to do. When I tried to change the plan, it was painful. Every part of me fought the change because I was going against my divine creation. And then, it happened. Epiphany. My life was in chaos. I was experiencing pain because I was no longer doing what I was designed to do. I had gotten away from my passion of working at the school and helping people every day. I had entered a chapter in life that was no longer filled with excitement or purpose. I was just going through the motions to make a living. I was lost and without hope because I was outside of my calling. When I stopped living my calling it hurt as much as taking air out of my lungs.

God created me with a purpose in mind for my life here on earth. He knew the plans He had for me all along and blessed me with the talent to accomplish those things. My job was to develop the skills and hone my craft, but He had already given me the talent. It makes total sense that I would experience discomfort when I wasn't doing what was inside of me to do. Then God began to show me His plan. It didn't happen overnight or all at once. The further I leaned into my relationship with Him, the less I felt my need to control the future, and the more I surrendered to His plan. This book, the podcast, the radio show, the social media posts, the life group, the speaking, and the coaching could not have happened until I got out of the way. It couldn't be about me, it had to be about God.

My story wasn't supposed to be one of many in a stack of tragic memoirs. God had plans for hope and a future. I have dreamed of speaking in front of women's groups, filled with women mourning the loss of dreams, the loss of loved ones, and the loss of innocence. I have prayed over the people I will meet who have broken foundations and lives filled with heartache. Every day I see people on social media who are paralyzed by anxiety, wiped out by depression, weighed down by stress, or lost in a dark pit of emotions. As I shifted my focus onto God's plan and my purpose, I began to burn with a sense urgency to reach hurting people.

CHAPTER SEVENTEEN

You Have Greatness Inside of You

In 2017, I developed a daily routine that changed my life. My search to find a glimmer of hope led me to listening to motivational videos on YouTube for at least an hour a day. Before I really knew how much I needed God, I knew I needed light. I recognized that I was in darkness, and I knew I needed help finding my way out. I discovered speakers who inspired me to take control of my life and become who I wanted to be. I played Eric Thomas and heard how successful people wake up early. I actually laughed out loud when I first started learning about the concept of waking up early and tackling my day with aggressive purpose. It was drastically different than the hostage negotiations I had with my alarm clock every single morning.

The alarm would scream at me relentlessly, and I would beg for mercy and ten more minutes before I had to face the world. Then, I would drag myself out of bed, throw something on, and head to the car. I fixed my hair and did my makeup on the way to work, finishing my eye liner and mascara in the parking lot before throwing on my shoes, grabbing my purse, and racing in at the last minute. Listening to Eric Thomas and Trent Shelton speak, I got the message: when your reality is better than your dreams, you won't have a problem waking up to face it.

The more I listened to speakers like Lisa Nicholas, Will Smith, Lewis Howes, and Tom Bilyeu, the more I understood that I was put on Earth for a purpose; I just had to get my life in order so I could fulfill it. In order to get where I wanted to go, I had to become the person I was supposed to be.

I could feel my mind changing through the transformation power of positivity. My desire to learn more about the power of the mind was insatiable. I listened to YouTube videos and podcasts on repeat. The messages began to shape the way I thought: *Don't give up. Keep going. Get up. Get in motion. Stop being negative. You will become what you dwell on. Validate yourself.* It was easy to embrace the concept of positive thinking, not even fully realizing that it was a Biblical principle. The concept didn't begin with Dale Carnegie or *The Secret*; it started long before that. Romans 12:2 says, "Don't become like the people of this world. Instead, change the way you think. Then you will always be able to determine what God really wants—what is good, pleasing, and perfect." (GOD'S WORD Translation)

My mission became to change my mind. Each time I finished listening to all the videos from one speaker, I moved on to the next, not even realizing how much I was allowing God to transform my mind. Compilation videos were played on repeat, and I took notes like I was studying for a class. Hope began to build inside of me. My thoughts began to change.

Soon, I began to connect those positive messages with Scriptures. God began working in my life to show me that Romans 8:28 was true, He *would* work all things together for His Glory. The scripture I had held onto for thirty years birthed new hope inside of me. I also clung to Jeremiah 29:11, which said God had a plan for me, to prosper me and not harm me, plans for a hope and a future. A future. I had honestly never thought about the future. I was in a trap of just surviving life. I was only reacting to crisis and riding a never-ending merry-go-round of chaos and turmoil. Sure, I would say, "One day, I want to..." or, "I wish I could..." but I hadn't really thought much about my actual future. Thankfully, God had.

My first epiphany came when I was listening to Les Brown speak on purpose. He continued to say, "You have greatness inside of you. You have greatness inside of you. You have greatness inside of you." A surge of energy began to build up inside of me as he spoke. I listened to the message and decided it was time to choose once and for all: life or death. I was at the crossroads where one path would take me to my destiny and the other would lead me to end my life. Something had to give.

I wanted to take the path that led to my destiny, but I was at the lowest of lows, struggling to find my purpose for living. I had lost sight of what my destiny even was. I was thirty-seven years old and faced the reality that I had failed in every area. Not only had I failed at all the things I had set out to accomplish, but I had compounded my failure by losing my identity in the process. I had quit everything I had ever started. I had rationalized my failures with whatever challenges had come my way. In truth, I didn't know how to truly fight for anything.

So, as Les Brown's voice kept repeating in my head, "There is greatness inside of you," I began to understand that my destiny was to be great. I wasn't fulfilled in my job because I was not seeing the reward of helping others transform their lives. My past experiences were not being utilized to help people in similar struggles. I felt lost. I knew I had overcome more in my life than any one person should have to. I knew that if I looked deep enough within, I would find greatness that I could share with others to help them through their own pain. That was my destiny.

My mother would testify that she has been fighting for my life since the day I was born. Whether it was health battles, abusive relationships, or my own choices that endangered my life, the fight has always been there. I went from crisis to tragedy, and then back to crisis again. I was so accustomed to dysfunction and drama that I was in a constant state of survival mode, waiting for the next crisis to deal with. In this hard world of survival of the fittest, there had to be a reason I was surviving, and one look in the mirror assured me that it was not because I was the fittest.

The question, "How am I still standing?" came to the forefront when I was listening to an Eric Thomas motivational video about the Lion and the Gazelle. In his message, Eric stated that if a gazelle is weak or sick, the lion won't attack it. If it didn't run, if it didn't pose a challenge, the lion wouldn't be interested. I viewed myself as weak and sickly. I reasoned that I had not been devoured by the world because I didn't pose a threat. The world was not interested in me. I thought about that as I got ready for the day. Brushing my teeth, I looked at myself in the mirror, unable to see a brave lion. I couldn't fathom that I was fierce, strong, or courageous.

In truth, the reason I hadn't achieved my dreams was because I didn't believe in my own strength and power. It wasn't about what had happened to me. It was about what I had done with it. God had not brought me through tragedy to merely survive life. God had called me to be a warrior. I had to learn that God wanted me to have a victorious and abundant life filled with joy and hope.

Standing in front of the mirror, facing my true self as honestly as possible, beyond the makeup and the smile, I tried to picture myself as a warrior. I thought about the words I had said to my son before every single football game he played during his nine years on the field. I would meet him at the fence—and even in high school, he'd make his way over within earshot—where I'd ask him one question, "What did God make you?" He would enthusiastically respond, "A warrior!" I saw tremendous strength in my child, but I failed to acknowledge my own strength, even though I had helped to instill strength in him.

I had to stop seeing myself through the lens of my past and start seeing my life as God intended it to be. God wasn't planning a Shakespearean tragedy for me, but He was able to use the tragedies He brought me through to help others with their own struggles. There are people I have been able to minister to that would not have received my message had I not walked through the same fire they were currently engulfed in.

As a young adult, I never felt worthy of a calling to ministry. Excuses and insecurities prohibited me from even trying. I felt like I was too broken to tell people how to be victorious. I wasn't talented enough or pretty enough to be on stage. I wasn't disciplined enough to finish writing a book. Stage fright prevented me from singing. I didn't have a college degree. I hadn't accomplished anything amazing enough to have a voice. Self-defeating thoughts captivated my mind, bound me up, and prevented me from running forward toward my destiny. I was stuck in the quicksand of shame and self-doubt.

My mom's wise words about merely accepting life and surviving came back to me, "You can either be a soldier fighting the war or a casualty. Which will it be?" My perception of myself certainly did not change overnight, but I was beginning to see myself differently. There was a small seed planted in mind which grew into a realization that I was created to conquer, not to be overtaken. It was time to stand up and fight for my mind. Even though I had spent my whole life in defense that I was not anyone's victim, I had trapped myself in a victim's mentality with a ready supply of excuses for failure and justification for giving up.

I spent enough time with myself, honestly reflecting in full transparency, to discover the parts of me that needed attention and healing. That's when I acknowledged that it was time to face the weak gazelle I had been, so I could become the courageous lion I wanted to be. It brought me full circle back to the reality that I was supposed to write my story. I needed to stop being paralyzed by fear of rejection so I could redefine my idea of success. By definition, success is achieving a goal. I couldn't say that I would write when I became successful. If my goal was to write, I couldn't be successful until I wrote my book. I was using my own self-doubt, "Who would possibly care what I have to say?" to stop me from sitting down and just writing.

Oh, I had great excuses. I didn't have a working computer. I didn't have time. I didn't have the money for an editor. I didn't know how to get published. I didn't have an audience. The truth is that while all of those were true, the real roadblock in my way was fear. I was scared to truly face my past and admit that it happened to me. I was terrified to stop telling my narrative as if I were a character in one of my stories and admit that I was the real person that all of those terrible things had happened to.

I made the decision to find a way to write my book, no matter what. Even when I didn't have a working computer at home. My first draft actually began with a stack of notebook paper and a pen in hand, just like I wrote my first stories back in the sixth grade. After all, people wrote books long before there were computers. I made the commitment to myself—*no more excuses*. I would write my story and see it through to the end.

The journey out of my own mind was filled with ups and downs, joy and sadness, pain and healing, and hate and forgiveness. I learned that I can't live my life in the pursuit of passion; I have to do it in the pursuit of purpose. Passion waivers with emotion, and I'd always quit trying whenever emotions changed. Once I became destiny driven, then I had to see it through until I reached my final destination, regardless of the roadblocks along the way.

CHAPTER EIGHTEEN

Broken Hearted

There was a moment in my life when I finally surrendered to God, and it started with the last time my heart got broken. In the summer of 2019, I had finally come to understand how much my dating choices were destroying me. I should have seen the heartbreak coming from years away. I had dated a guy off and on for fifteen years, more off than on, if I'm honest. We met at work and started an affair many years ago, in 2003. He was married, and I wasn't. I justified it that I wasn't looking for love or a commitment. Oh how wrong I was about it all. When my feelings began to get involved, I ended it. I married another man shortly after we broke up and thought I'd never see the guy again. However, we stayed in touch here and there. After my divorce, he reappeared in my life, seemingly when I needed him most. I thought it was fate, when really it was a lack of security settings on my Facebook profile that made my posts visible, thereby sending out the beacon that I was needy, lonely, and desperate.

We never dated again until after his divorce, although I saw him a few times through the years. Had anyone tried to tell me he was using me, I would have said they were crazy, that he really cared about me. He'd come and go in my life, until after his divorce in 2018. After his marriage ended, I had been single for a long time. We started talking and spending more time together. Anyone who was around us loved us together. People stopped us when we were walking and told us we made a cute couple. We planned a future together, and we proclaimed our love. I dreamed of what it would be like to finally be with him. I allowed my heart to hope. He disappeared from my life for months at a time, but I always let him talk his way back in.

When we talked, it was perfect, it was everything I could have asked for in a relationship. However, after intimacy, he'd disengage from me for several days. I had brought it up as a concern but he always denied it. On the final night I saw him, he called me and asked me to come over. He let me know that nothing else would get in the way of us finally being together. He said everything I had longed to hear for fifteen years. I hesitated. I told him I wasn't ready to be intimate with him, expressing my fear of him disengaging again. He assured me he wasn't going anywhere. After I arrived, it became clear quickly that his expectation was for us to have sex. I set aside my own personal feelings and did what I was expected to do. Just like I always did. He called me the next day, told me he loved me, and asked if he could call me later. He then blocked my number, blocked me on all social media, and never spoke to me again.

I was devastated. I had so many unanswered questions. I felt foolish, used, and rejected. I made a decision that it would be the last time that something like that would happen to me. I had to stop the cycle of making bad choices about men. I had to stop talking to men who used me. I had to establish healthy boundaries. I made a two-year commitment to God. I devoted a full two years to not seeing anyone romantically and focusing on my relationship with God, setting healthy boundaries, and fulfilling God's calling on my life.

As someone whose identity had been so closely connected to sexuality, I struggled through the first few months of being intentionally single. There were a few men in my life I had to completely stop talking to, a couple of exes that would have been a prime safety net for compromise. I had no idea how much God would use that time in my life to heal my mind and restore my heart.

When I chose abstinence for the first time in my adult life, I discovered a new price tag on my self-worth. By putting my relationship with God before any desire I felt physically, mentally, or emotionally, I learned how to have healthy, fulfilling relationships in my life. After a year of being intentionally single, I met some really amazing friends, and I was more prepared for that friendship because of the time I had dedicated to God. I had finally repaired the cracks in my foundation and grounded my self-worth in Christ.

I also created a standard for any future relationships I may have. I wish I had learned this hard lesson long before my fortieth birthday, but I am worth waiting for. Who I am as a person deserves both love and acceptance. What I do does not define who I am, and I am worth getting to know. Even more, I am worth someone who loves God more the they love their flesh. If I am seeking a man of God who will put God first, I won't find that in someone who makes their most important decisions based on desire.

CHAPTER NINETEEN

A Father's Love

Before I could accept God as my Father, and thereby contemplate His love for me as genuine and lasting, I had to reconcile how I felt about my biological father. I forced myself to explore memories of him beyond tragedy or violation. I reached out to members of my family who had good memories of him and loved him deeply. I didn't want to only remember a monster. I wanted to remember the man I loved as my dad before he crushed me. I took time to remember his talents, musicianship, and storytelling.

Clearly, he suffered from mental illness and was an unstable person. I have accepted that he had deep-rooted character flaws that led to him perpetuating generational curses and cycles of abuse. I acknowledged the past for what it was and accepted the facts without venom because I released the toxicity of hate.

As I continued to navigate the path toward freedom in my life, I had to open myself up to spiritual discovery by reconciling my beliefs about God and faith. I kept seeking answers and learning about Him until I had a solid understanding of the loving nature of God and how He felt about me. I began to understand that He viewed me as His precious daughter.

Restoring my faith required me to confront my doubts and ask the questions I was ashamed to ask. God never rejected me in my doubts or brokenness. He met me right where I was and embraced me as the child He had been waiting on to return home. I didn't understand the unfailing, unwavering love of a parent until I was a parent.

It was in the depths of my love for my own son that I discovered the depths of a "no matter what" kind of love. I have been pretty mad my son at various times in his life, like the time when he was in the sixth grade and got spray paint all over my car. I was furious, but I didn't stop loving him. Or the time he had a pellet gun war in my house with a few of his friends who had spent the night, and I woke up to 5,000 pellets all over my living room. I was livid, but I didn't stop loving him.

Every time I encountered one of those moments with him that tested my patience, I gained a better understanding of how God loved me. Part of my spiritual battle was rooted in shame. I felt like I had let God down time and time again—like the dozens of times I allowed the wrong guy into my life, and I completely derailed my plans because he temporarily satisfied my emotional needs. God picked up the pieces of my broken heart while I cried about being used and abandoned yet again. I can only imagine the level of "What are you doing?" God must have felt when I wasn't a good steward of what He blessed me with.

There were times when I left jobs too soon, or moved on to seemingly bigger, better deals, and times I didn't trust Him to take care of me, allowing panic to prompt negative decisions instead. I carried those regrets around in a backpack of emotions, constantly strapped to my back. I chose shame. I was the one who wouldn't let go of the negativity. God had already forgiven me when I repented and took steps to correct my behavior. God never quit on me, even though I gave him every reason to.

BOND with me here on a harsh reality and supremely honest confession. I was *terrible* at breaking promises to God. How awful is that to say out loud? I did though. Just like I would tell myself that I was going to start a diet, and then throw the plan out the window, I would do that with God. With Him, it would be more like promising to wake up early to spend time in prayer, or committing to a reading plan, then not following through. What about fasting? Have you ever tried fasting because everyone in your church was doing it, only you didn't have a real conviction about it, so it lasted about six hours before you were ready to eat everything in sight? Have you ever stopped going to a church that you were once a big part of because you got offended, even though you committed to God and that ministry that you'd be there long-term? Have you ever started planning out something God put on your heart but never saw it through? *Asking for a friend.* Yeah, I am a friend. I'm asking for me. I did all of that. I really wish I hadn't, but I did, and I had to unpack all of that into the very capable arms of my Savior who died on the cross so that I didn't have to carry the regrets around in my backpack anymore.

I have scars tied to my past choices and regrets. I stood before God, remorseful about the times I made promises to Him but didn't keep my word. Yet with a love that is almost unfathomable, God never stopped loving me. He never stopped trusting me. He remained patient and kind. He forgave me unconditionally. Even though I failed Him, He never, ever, ever failed me.

God knew the state of my heart. He knew that I struggled with my faith to the point that I wasn't sure if I identified as a Christian or Agnostic. I wasn't sure if I believed in God as He was presented by the Church. I wasn't sure that we, as flawed humans with finite minds, could comprehend God. I still don't think we truly understand the magnitude of Him, but God accepted me with open arms and healed the wounds I experienced when I embarked on the lonely, shame-filled journey of questioning my faith.

During that time, I was looking for a safe, judgement-free place to ask my questions and voice my doubts. I was desperate for someone to embrace me in love and kindness and listen while I confessed the thoughts that filled me with shame when I said them out loud. I needed someone to help me find answers. Not only did God gently guide me toward Truth and embrace me right where I was, but He also put a burden on my heart to love His people right where they are, doubts and all. I hope that we as a Church get to a place that we embrace healthy questioning. In all of the scriptures I have ever read, I have never once seen Jesus tell someone, "Hey, we don't talk about that." He never chastised someone for asking a heart-felt question. Rather, He made time to meet people where they were. He made the effort to meet me where I was.

I had to root my beliefs in what God thought and said about me. I was allowed to ask Him questions, and He was never going to turn around and say, "I was going to do this, but you asked Me too many questions. Never mind." God isn't moved by my fears or doubts. I can't break Him. It's not possible to be so messed up that He doesn't want me. It's impossible for me to reach out to Him and in response, He turns his back on me. Those beliefs, if given root, would only rob me of hope and keep me silent when what I really needed was to cry out to my Father.

Here's another BONDing moment: God is not changed by my questions or doubts. When I finally accepted that God wants a relationship with me, it was pivotal. I had never realized that He *actually wanted* to reveal Himself to me beyond my limited vision of Him as the Creator of the Universe. He wanted me to embrace Him as *my* Creator, *my* Father, *my* Friend, *my* Savior and *my* Redeemer. I had no idea that He wanted open dialogue. God hates anything that causes us to hide from Him. The "off-limits" topics that hindered my relationship with God were preventing me from living in full peace.

I learned to talk to God about sadness, depression, and anxiety. I learned to be real with God. It was liberating. I needed more than a half-hearted "I'll pray for you" or a bumper-sticker-worthy cliché like "Let Go and Let God." I needed tangible strategies. I found those strategies when I became open and honest with God as my Father. God knows my heart, my passions, my quirks, and my fears. He does not expect me to go through life stoically. He knows that I don't live in a perfect Utopia and that I don't always feel love, joy, and happiness all the time.

When I realized that God had designed me to grow through the obstacles, I became less afraid to talk to Him about the feelings and real-life struggles I experienced while hurdling those barriers. I stopped shying away from exploring unanswered questions or mysteries I couldn't explain. I got to know God as real and relevant. I finally acknowledged that He loved me and accepted me as I am.

I rebuilt my faith from square one, not basing it on what I had always heard in church or what family members taught me, but by learning who God is for myself. I couldn't inherit my family's faith. I could learn stories passed down from generations, I could learn songs and memorize scriptures, but the mechanics did not replace the relationship. I couldn't inherit a relationship with God. I had to discover Him on my own.

CHAPTER TWENTY

The Most Beautiful Final Breath

I believe that the most powerful human emotion is disappointment. When what we expect to happen is not what actually happens, it can drive us to react in a way that is completely out of character. Here's an example: when I was at the gym, and I heard someone say that I was fat, it hurt my feelings, mostly because it touched on one of my insecurities. But I didn't leave the gym because of it. I was fully expecting to be judged about my size by super-fit people around me at the gym. And while most people didn't seem to notice me, there was one person I overheard say something intentionally cruel about me. While that stung, I wasn't devastated by his words because they were in line with my expectations. However, when I experienced cruel words from members of my church, I was crushed. Not only was I crushed, but I carried those painful words with me for a very long time. Mostly, I think I was disappointed because of *who* said it, even more than the sting of what they said. I felt blindsided, and what I expected from that person didn't match the reality of what really went down. I reacted in complete defensiveness because of the power of disappointment.

There was a powerful distinction, though, that took me years to process. I was not disappointed in Christ; I was disappointed in a Christian. It would have been easy to question their faith and ministry and to remove grace from the equation of forgiveness. That isn't how God operates though. I judged a person based on one of their lowest moments and allowed it to build up inside of me as resentment, which became the lens through which I viewed their whole life. The choice to hold onto negativity impacted me profoundly, but the person who made the hurtful remark never even knew I was upset. I don't think they ever knew I found out about what they said. Staying mad at him was exhausting. Dodging him in the busy hallways at church and plastering on a smile felt disingenuous, hypocritical and forced *because it was.*

Matthew 11:28-30 (AMP) states, "Come to Me, all who are weary and heavily burdened [by religious rituals that provide no peace], and I will give you rest [refreshing your souls with salvation]. Take My yoke upon you and learn from Me [following Me as My disciple], for I am gentle and humble in heart, and you will find rest (renewal, blessed quiet) for your souls."

I was weary and burdened by religious rituals that provided me no peace. I was church-scarred from being talked about, judged, and rejected. I was going to Sunday services out of obligation and fear of what would happen if I broke that routine. I was looking for a church where I could engage and be accepted. I wanted more than, "You are welcome here;" I wanted, "You belong here." I desperately wanted to contribute to God's Kingdom. Serving God started when I genuinely laid down my past hurts, guilt, and shame, and followed Jesus as His disciple. I accepted Him as gentle and humble in heart and ever true to His word, and just like He promised, He gave me rest. He renewed me. I learned to have peace in the blessed quiet of my soul.

I had a foundation of faith, but my foundation was broken. I knew what the Scriptures said, I just didn't internalize how they applied to me. I had a lot of ideas about God that were all wrong because I had a lot of ideas about love and relationships that were all wrong. Moving past the church scars was more about facing my own choices and lack of maturity in handling difficult situations than it was about confronting others who hurt me with their thoughtlessness. I had to be honest with myself about how deeply the words and actions of others hurt me. I felt like I had two choices about past pain: confront it or get over it. Continuing to carry the past around with me had to stop being an option. I had to change my perspective so I could change how I perceived God and His people. Since I had a broken foundation of faith, and because the person who taught me most about God had violated my trust in the worst way, my vision was blurred. I needed spiritual glasses.

My quest to discover God started in Genesis, mostly because "In the beginning" made a lot of sense to me as a starting point. Almost immediately, I had questions. I had questions about Adam sinning and why God asked Adam what he'd done. I gained more answers than I had questions for. The first revelation I had about God was that He created me and He loves me. That may sound simple, but it wasn't easy for me to accept.

I knew I had to hand Him all of my fears and doubts. I wanted to find a way to cast my cares on Him and to accept that He cares for me (1 Peter 5:7). But before I could do that, I had to turn over all of the guilt, shame, regret, anxiety, fear, and burden to Him. An emotional collapse came one day as I sat in the floor and poured my heart out to God. I finally gave voice to the thoughts that had been locked away for more than two decades. In the midst of the tears, I finally asked the burning question I felt so guilty for having, "God, I know that people have free will, I get that. But what I don't understand is how a man who prayed, who prophesied, and who had an anointed ministry could do the things he did to me. How could You use him when he was such a horrible person?"

There was no clarity or a clear word from God at that time. That moment was more about God listening to me as I broke. I yelled and cried and apologized and rehearsed tragedies. As I emptied my heart of the negativity, I began to feel a weight lift from my shoulders. In my sorrow, I found peace. I opened my heart to start the process of healing. I began to learn how to forgive myself and found ways to forgive those who had hurt me. It was time to move past the horrible memories and find a way to forgive. I didn't ultimately choose to forgive because others deserved my forgiveness. It wasn't because they apologized. It was because I needed peace. I forgave them so they would no longer have power in my life. I forgave them so I could be made whole and finally accept who I was and how God saw me.

In everything God created, He was pleased. Genesis 1:4 (NIV) **"God saw that the light was good."** Genesis 1:10 (NIV) "God called the dry ground land...**And God saw that it was good.**" Genesis 1:12 (NIV) "The land produced vegetation...**And God saw that it was good."** Genesis 1:18 "...and separated the light from darkness. **And God saw that it was good."** Genesis 1:25, "God made wild animals...**And God saw that it was good."** Genesis 1: 31 (NIV) God saw all that he had made, **and it was very good**."

I was created perfectly by the very same God Who created the universe, and I am good. Admitting to myself that I was innately good because I was created in the image of God was a challenge. That realization was connected to an understanding that God had a plan and purpose for creating me. His purpose did not change because of abuse or trauma. I am not alone. I am loved. I am worthy. I have every right to have a healthy, loving, fulfilling relationship with my Father in Heaven. I *can* be made whole. I have been forgiven. I haven't fallen too far from grace for God to reach me because God does not define His love for me by my actions, good or bad. God created me, and if He is proud of His creation, then I should be too.

When I lived emotionally, I inadvertently tethered myself to my past pain and to those who had caused me pain. They became the weight on my shoulders and the voices of doubt in my mind. It was time to evict the bad tenants who occupied space in my mind and fill that space with the people and thoughts that would help me fully achieve my purpose.

Many of the scriptures in Genesis answered my most basic questions about the nature and character of God. In the beginning, God created the world by speaking it into existence. Every time I am out in nature observing the intricate ecosystem of our planet, I am reaffirmed that it could not have happened by chance. Every time I visit the doctor and consider how the systems of the body depend upon one another and operate in perfect unison, I know that we are His labor of love. God created Adam in His own image. The creation of man was God's beautiful handiwork. In Genesis 2:7 (NIV), the Bible tells us that "God formed a man from the dust of the ground and breathed into his nostrils the breath of life, and the man became a living being." I can't help but think about my son in the delivery room. The nurse held him, and I waited anxiously to hear his first breath. There was painful silence for just a moment, and the thoughts whirled in my head, "Is he okay?" Suddenly he gasped for air and let out a wail that let all within earshot know that he had arrived. In one perfect moment, he transitioned from being completely dependent on my womb for life and nutrients to suddenly breathing on his own. It was time for his place in this world to begin, and it started with great relief when he took his first breath of air.

I had the honor of witnessing my son take his first breath as he entered the world, and in July 2019 I had the honor of being by my grandfather's side as he drew his last. Here's the beauty of how God works: literally every other person who visited hospice those final days talked about Grandad giving them a foundation of faith. I hadn't told anyone I was struggling deeply with my faith. I had desperately cried out for God to show me that He was real and that I mattered to Him. I wanted Him to show me that I was still His and that He loved me.

I have a history of pulling away from loved ones at the end of their life, but everything was different with my grandfather, I made an intentional decision to be as close to him as possible during those last days. Instead of saying my goodbyes and distancing myself, I made sure that my time and attention were on his needs. My focus had shifted from how I could prepare myself for pain and loss to how I could serve him and usher him into his eternity, making his final days as precious as possible. I had lost people close to me, but I think what made it so different with Grandad was that he was a part of my everyday life, habits, and routines. He had lived in the same house as us for some time, and during the final eight months of his life, I only lived a couple of blocks away.

At the beginning of June, shortly after his 83rd birthday, my dad came home from running errands and found my grandfather in the floor. Because he was too heavy for my dad to lift alone, Dad called me so Country could help him lift Grandad. We jumped into the car and rushed down the street. As soon as my dad and Country lifted my grandfather, I knew he had suffered a stroke. I could tell in the way he moved. I called 9-1-1 and rode with him in the ambulance to the hospital, watching his every movement, uncertain what his future would hold. I tried to hang onto his hand as long as I could. At the hospital, they discovered a large area in his brain that had been impacted by the stroke. At first he was rehabbing well. He fought hard to regain strength and full use of the left side of his body.

Then he had a series of setbacks, most likely due to a second stroke. By July, when he reached a point that he could no longer eat or drink, he was placed in hospice care. I left work on a Tuesday, telling my boss that he'd be gone by Friday. I didn't know at the time that hospice was predicting that he would have two weeks left to live; I just knew that God was preparing my heart that the end was near. I sat by his bed those last few days, praying that he wouldn't suffer. I sang soft hymns to him and held his hand, memorizing as much as I could about the lines on his hands and the veins, and the way his hand felt in mine.

He was completely lucid until after my brother arrived from Oklahoma at 9:00 PM Thursday evening. My brother, an ordained minister, thanked my grandfather for his life and all he had taught him. They shared memories. We all laughed together and tried not to cry in front of him much. As the night went on, his breathing changed, and we knew the end was close. I was in the hall with my sister while my mom spent a few precious moments with her dad. She came running into the hall and said, "Get a nurse. He stopped breathing." My sister ran for the nurse, and I rushed into the room and sat on the edge of my grandfather's bed next to him.

His breathing had started again as quickly as it had stopped. He looked anxiously around the room. First to my mom, his rock. Then over at my sister, who had returned with the nurse. And then, in one beautiful moment, he locked eyes with me. He was restless at first, until I took his face in my hands and said, "It's okay. Everything is going to be okay." And then his eyes looked beyond me, and I saw the most beautiful, spiritual encounter I have ever witnessed. There was a split second of brightness in his eyes and his face lit up, and then he was gone. Just like that. I saw the light go from his eyes, I knew he had crossed into heaven. I couldn't question it or doubt it because the gift that God had given me was that I *saw* it happen.

Up to that moment I would have told you that I was not one hundred percent sure what happened when someone died. There are so many conflicting doctrinal beliefs, and I have always avoided theological debates that didn't change anything about my walk with God. I had accepted that I didn't have to know the answer to that question. At that time, I was struggling with my faith on a deeper level. But in one moment, I received the most beautiful gift that God could have given me. Peace. I could never again question what happens next because for just an instant, I saw it.

I physically saw my grandfather transition into the afterlife. My mom and sister witnessed the same thing. There was a clear moment that he saw the other side. There was a clear moment that he locked eyes with me, and in a twinkling of an eye, he was gone. That split

second was enough to tell me without another doubt ever
that God is real. Heaven is real. There is something
beyond this life we live. God, the perfect Creator of the
Universe, is Who He says He is.

CHAPTER TWENTY-ONE:

My Own Story to Tell

I think back to before Jesus died on the cross, when He was in the Garden praying, "God if it be Your will, take this cup from me." How many things in my life did I pray for God to take away from me because they seemed bigger than what I could endure? God's answer was often *no*. I had to walk through trials. It's not that God doesn't care what I want, but rather God's ways are perfect. In order to become who I was called to be, I had to get out of His way and trust that He knew a whole lot more than I did. I couldn't allow my ego, opinions, agendas or emotions to alter what He was trying to do. Even with this book, I knew that I wasn't really ready to write it.

When I started writing the book in 2017-2018, I was extremely close friends with a man we'll call the Mentor. The Mentor was a brilliant man with a business mind unlike any I had ever seen. He was one of the first male friends I had that I didn't date. However, I was enamored with his knowledge on life and business. I sought to please him more than any person in my past. Our relationship was toxic with wild swings from high to low.

He taught me about Dale Carnegie; he taught me about *The Secret* and putting things into the universe that you want returned to you; and he taught me about websites and marketing. He encouraged me to finish my book before taking on anything new, but I didn't listen. At that time, I thought I could take on the world and hold it all together. I was doing a weekly radio show; Country was sick; and I was trying to single-handedly pull off a women's conference. To say it was a disaster would be a huge understatement. I let a lot of people down and had to refund everyone's money out of my own pocket. I cancelled speakers and vendors. It was awful. I crashed and burned.

The Mentor was so angry that in our final conversation, he said, "I just wanted to help you. I believed in you."

I replied, "Did you? Or did you just believe in your ability to make me great?"

He was crushed by my statement, which was not my intention, but it was the truth of how I really felt. I felt like I had become his version of me and that I had lost my true self in the mix. I was ready to write a book about getting out of my own mind when I had basically jumped into his. When I would sit down to write the parts of the book that were hard to talk about, I froze. I couldn't make myself write them. I couldn't figure out what I wanted to say. I had complete writer's block.

I was only focused on freedom and empowerment. I was focused on giving a voice to survivors. I wanted to be a Lisa Nichols, Rachel Hollis, Mel Robbins, or Brené Brown. Each of these dynamic "sheroes" had impacted my life and inspired me to return to the dream of writing and speaking. Each of these powerful ladies were trailblazers for everything I was trying to accomplish in my life. They had taught me how to identify my issues, deal with toxic thinking, and remove roadblocks from my life that were preventing me from reaching my true purpose (or as Lisa Nichols says, "my life assignment").

What I failed to see was that my job wasn't to be an extension of their greatness, but to be great. I wasn't meant to redeliver their messages. In my eagerness to follow their path, I had forgotten that I had my own unique story and message in my personal journey to live the life I was created to live.

I forgot about the people who might need to hear what I have to say. It was okay that my life purpose included an overtly faith-based message. Each of those "sheroes" spoke of their own belief system, but their focus was on practical advice and real solutions for people who had deep rooted struggles. Their messages appealed to the masses. I was terrified that I wouldn't have my own message to share, and if I wasn't unique, why would anyone want to listen to me? I carried The Mentor's voice in my mind, "Who are you? Why would anyone want to listen to anything you have to say? You're nobody." I didn't want to stand in front of a crowd with the message, "Everything Mel Robbins said—and Jesus." A beautiful thing happened though. Once I surrendered and just said, "Okay God, I will do the work. I will study, I will dig deeper, and I will listen for what You are trying to say through me," then it all came together.

I was missing the part about bringing hope to the hopeless. I was forgetting about those who were just like me who were in the Church and feeling lost. I forgot that we don't talk about depression and anxiety in a safe way inside the Church. I forgot about being the person sitting in a chair on Sunday morning feeling like I just didn't fit in because I wasn't like the other women around me. I forgot about the warriors who were battling as they tried to reconcile their past with their faith. I forgot that I wasn't the only one who sat in church with scars from self-harm or the beautiful warriors who were battle-weary with pending plans to end their life. I forgot I wasn't the only one who drove to church with tears running down her face as I cried out to God to speak to me that day and give me one small thing to cling to that would save me. What about those who had been hurt in the Church and had made their pain synonymous with their view of Christianity? I would have failed every single person who read my book if I shared empowerment, but neglected to help them restore their faith, because that wasn't my message to share.

That doesn't negate the life changing messages that started me on my healing journey that came from amazing works like *Girl, Wash Your Face* and *Girl, Stop Apologizing* by Rachel Hollis, where I was called out of my habits and into motivation to become a better version of myself. *Daring Greatly* by Brené Brown taught me how to be open and vulnerable in a positive way. Lisa Nichols' book *No Matter What* changed my life. She taught me to say *no* and use it as a full sentence. These women wrote about real challenges that helped me take charge of my life.

My journey is a bit different though. I still want to give voice to those who were silenced and to help people tell the stories that have been locked up inside of them for far too long. However, my story must start with the healing and reprogramming process that helped me take my life back.

CHAPTER TWENTY-TWO

Empowered Within

Over the last five years of coaching, I have had the honor or helping numerous clients identify their strengths and develop an action plan to achieve their goals. Around the time I started coaching, a big buzz word on social media was *empowerment*. By definition *empowerment is authority or power given to someone to do something; the process of becoming stronger and more confident, especially in controlling one's life and claiming one's rights.* Admittedly, it sounds pretty cool to be able to empower someone to do something they didn't think they could do. However, when I read the definition of empowerment as it applied to my own life, my first thought was that a coach couldn't empower me because they didn't hold power over me in the first place. They couldn't give me power that I already contained, but just wasn't accessing. I didn't need anyone else's permission to be who I was called to be. God empowered me. He equipped me, called me, prepared me, anointed me, and then empowered me. That mind-blowing realization changed my entire coaching philosophy.

I can best describe that conversation with God as Him gently telling me to stay in my lane. Much like the revelation He gave me that it wasn't my job to heal broken hearts, neither was it my job to give people power. That is His job. My calling entails helping people discover the power that God has already given them. I get to help my clients by being their biggest fan, identifying obstacles, brainstorming action plans, holding them accountable, and offering tough love as needed. What an honor to be a part of that process. I get to be the coach and the trainer who prepares them for the big game. I also get to be the loudest cheerleader on the sidelines as they take the field and play for their life.

After I have really gotten to know a new client and what stage of life they are in, I dive right in to the hard stuff. Every single one of my clients is asked this series questions to help me identify where their purpose and passions lie:

1. *What's the end goal of your life?*
2. *What is it that you would do if money wasn't a factor?*
3. *If we were standing at your Celebration of Life, what would you want people to be celebrating and remembering about you?*

I start there because of some common threads I have found with clients who struggle with anxiety and/or depression, or those who are miserable in life. The first component is that they have lost their sense of purpose or stepped away from their calling. While the path is different for every person I have worked with, the common thread is that they are no longer finding intrinsic fulfillment in their day-to-day activities.

Together we explore the forgotten dreams or the ones they gave up on, like when I accepted the lie that I just wasn't the "forever girl" and gave up on having a healthy, happy relationship. I had a long list of faults that I accepted as evidence for my conclusion. I didn't view it as giving up; I saw it as being honest with myself. Looking back through a 20/20 lens, I can see that it was a defense mechanism I created to shield my heart from future rejection by changing my expectations.

There were, of course, other dreams I had given up on, not just relationship goals. I remember the longing I felt when reading books. The desire to write my own tugged at my heartstrings. I envisioned my writing career in great detail, from the serene places I would write to the bookshelves my books would sit on in stores. I could see myself at a signing table with pen in hand, greeting readers, and praying with them. It was the same way with speaking. I would envision myself traveling to speaking engagements, standing on the stage, looking out over a crowd. I could picture exercises we'd do together and hear words I would say. I could picture the face of a woman I was supposed to pray over. It wasn't just a dream or "what if," it was God's purpose for my life, and it called to me.

Early in my career in education, I was the Redirection Aide. Redirection was a program in our school that helped students who struggled with behavior. My main focus was to help students learn the skills needed to be successful in the classroom. I loved that role! I got to experience classrooms in a new way. I had a great group of students with whom I worked every day. Often, if a teacher had to step out of their classroom for any reason, I would cover their room for them. One particular day, a teacher had an emergency meeting about one of her students, and I entered the room just in time to transition the students to the carpet for our group discussion. (I'll change the names in the story for privacy's sake.)

Mrs. Smith's first-grade classroom was decorated neatly, and everything was in order as a fun group of energetic kids made their way to the carpet for a discussion about Martin Luther King, Jr. After reading a story to them, we all sat in a circle as each child took turns telling their own dream. "When I grow up, I want to be a doctor!" "When I grow up, I want to be a baseball player!" "I'm going to be a teacher!" I focused on each student and was impressed with their answers. I had kind of feared answers like my friend's son who desperately wanted to be a crash test dummy when he grew up. But one by one, all the way around the room and eighteen students later, we ended with Hannah.

Sweet, beautiful, fidgety Hannah, with the weight of the world on her shoulders and sorrows the depth of the ocean in her eyes. She proudly announced, "When I grow up, I am going to be a UNICORN!!!" The other kids laughed. Hannah ducked her head; a lock of her blonde hair fell in front of her face. I cringed and gave the angry mom look that silenced snickers. One overly helpful student said, "Unicorns aren't real!" To Hannah, those were fighting words. She pushed the strands away and fiercely said, "They are real, and I'm going to be one. I am going to fly around the rainbows, and I'm going to save all the boys and girls that need help." Her critics grew silent, I think it was mostly because of her conviction. One student timidly asked, "Ms. Cook, *are* unicorns real?"

I had a decision to make. I knew that Hannah desperately needed to hold onto something. Her life was in shambles and she was not equipped to handle the kind of pressures that would make many adults buckle. Because of my work with her, I knew the struggles that she was facing from her past and the horrific memories that haunted her. It wasn't my job to give her a reality check; it was my job to help her find strength within her while maintaining honesty and integrity in the process. *Talk about a balancing act.* I took a quick breath, and gave her small hand a squeeze. Standing up and pulling her with me, I proudly announced, "You know what I believe? I believe that if *anyone* in the whole wide world," exaggerating my words to capture everyone's attention, "is brave enough and creative enough to become a unicorn and save the world, it is Hannah! In fact, I think..." I leaned in closer, propping my hands on my knees, and the students leaned in to hear what was next. "I think that Hannah should write a story about it! Let's all write stories about how cool it will be when our dreams come true!"

Luckily, it worked. Throughout the year, Hannah wrote many stories in which she became a beautiful, strong unicorn who said all of the things she wasn't ready to say in real life and battled the people she wanted to battle who had hurt her. She found her voice. Sound familiar? It was exactly, in a much simpler way, what Mrs. Pilgrim did for me in the sixth grade.

The start of dreaming again is often the catalyst for my clients to remember their purpose. The answer to the question, "What was your dream before someone else told you that it could never happen?" became a beacon of hope for many of my clients to return to. I mean, I'll be the first to break it to you that if you are an adult who is planning on becoming a unicorn, then this journey might need to start with some of my famous Mama Cook tough love. Other than that, I believe that the possibilities of what we can achieve are endless if we are willing to do the work.

There is a scene in the movie *Sister Act 2* where Whoopi Goldberg's character, Sister Mary Clarence, tells Lauren Hill's character, Rita, that "if you wake up in the morning and you can't think of anything but singing first, then you're supposed to be a singer, girl." It was the nagging desires tugging on my heart strings to speak, write, and coach that caused me to take action. I felt like I owed it to myself, and anyone else God wanted to reach through me, to at least try. There was an emptiness inside of me that I just couldn't fill with anything else, and I tried!

Creative expression was the second component of getting out of my own mind, and it's the second insight I look at with my coaching clients. While writing and speaking may be talents that are part of my divine destiny, there are other skills that may not be. For example, I can secretly sing. Very secretly. I have the ability, and I love to sing in private, but I am miserable singing on stage. I know I am not called to be a singer. However, singing is a form of creative expression for me.

There were times in my life that I didn't have any words to say to God. That usually happened during times that I was hurting deeply or when I was in the process of healing. I wasn't angry or pouting, I just didn't have anything to say. I can remember going into a quiet place in my home, turning on worship music, and whispering, "God I don't have any words of my own right now, but I want you to know that I mean the words of this song with all of my heart." Worship became my lifeline to God. It is incredibly important to me, it's just not part of my career path. I don't have to stop singing or minimize its importance in my life just because it isn't part of my big picture. It is a creative outlet. Worship is still my personal way to express my heart to God.

I find that many of my clients have lost creative expression. When I am diving deeper with them about this topic, I find out their talents, hobbies, and the things they once loved, but stopped doing years ago. Then comes the first of many challenges I ask of them, "Will you trust me enough to share your talent with me? Right here, right now." Nervous excitement inevitably follows. The answer is not always *yes* the first time; sometimes we have to remove some obstacles of doubt or insecurity to uncover the courage it takes to share something personal. When it does happen though, the results are honest, vulnerable, and magical. I have seen dances, songs, poems, stories, and beautiful paintings come to life from the deepest part of someone's creative space. I have seen architectural drawings, fashion sketches, and home décor designs. I have seen scrapbooks, graphic designs, and computer development. I have heard instruments played, songs written, songs sung, and people give moving speeches that brought me to tears. Outside of singing, my creative expression is writing and speaking. Those two outlets are tied directly to my calling as an author, speaker, and coach. I don't have to focus on only one of them because they are all in alignment. One message with multiple delivery methods.

Developing my destiny required identifying my purpose and combining it with some of my creative expressions: *yes to writing, no to singing.* Then, I developed a plan that centered around one question, "What problem am I going to provide a solution for?" My entire business plan centered around reaching out to people who were hurting and helping them figure out the "and, then." What I call the "and, then" is acknowledging tragedy that happened, then focusing on the next steps. I help my clients unpack the burdens they carry and expose the skeletons in their closet, "and, then" we start a plan of action to leave those skeletons behind as they move forward to fulfill their destiny.

CHAPTER TWENTY-THREE

Roadblocks

It's never as simple as just figuring out what someone wants to do or feels called to do. There are usually roadblocks such as insecurity, unhealed wounds, or unforgiveness that stop a person from pursuing their calling. Forgiveness fosters healing and unleashes power within.

One of my own personal roadblocks was learning to release the venom I felt toward my biological father, exes, or other people I felt had wronged me. I changed my connotation with forgiveness from the warped perception that to forgive meant to let go and never bring it up again to a healthier perspective that forgiveness means I have released the grip that my past and the past choices of specific people had on my life. I accepted that forgiveness does not erase consequences for actions, but that it does free me from having to dictate what those consequences are. When God began to reestablish my connection with the concept of forgiveness, I wrote this journal entry.

I don't forgive you because you deserve it...I forgive you because I am not willing to give you power over me anymore.
I refuse to rent out space in my mind to those who devalue it. I refuse to bring hurt or hate with me on my journey forward while leaving you in the past.
You set out to destroy me and bring me down to your level. You failed at both. You may have victimized me in the past, but I am not your victim any longer.

*I didn't walk away from you...I ran...And the gold
medal in that track event will hang in the trophy case of
my life from this day forward.
I used to think that I couldn't escape your hold on me,
but I am free.
You will not be my excuse to fail...
Because I will not fail.
You will not be the name of my pain...
Because I am whole.
I used to wish you harm
But now I don't wish you anything at all.
My life is not defined by whether or not justice is
served. I release you fully to God.
On this day, I let you go. I. Forgive. You.*

Forgiveness is the most powerful weapon I have to destroy the past's grip on my future. By choosing to forgive, I released the power within me to move away from what happened to me, while unburdening the weight of sorrow and shame I had carried since I was nine years old. My biological father's actions always seemed unforgiveable to me. Not only the abuse, but I was angry that he took the easy way out and left me to deal with the aftermath alone. I warred inside with being the only one who had consequences for his actions. I held on so tightly to my emotional response that year by year it only grew heavier because I added more emotional baggage to it. I found peace in finally coming to terms with the fact that no matter how hard I hung onto anger or hate, it didn't change the outcome of what happened.

I look back at what my life was like when I was having panic attacks every day, and I see the enormous weight I carried. I picture myself wearing a backpack like the ones hikers wear when they are preparing to climb a mountain. However, instead of it being filled with supplies, food, and water that would help me on my journey, it was filled with the weights I had picked up along the path. Some of the weights were heavier than others, depending on the level of pain I associated with a person or event. In this imaginary journey, I just kept climbing the mountain, as other hikers came by and crammed another weight in my backpack. I think of how different it would have been to have walked with God, Who would have taken those weights for me. I also think that it would have been great if I had I taken the "I don't want your stinking weight!" approach and not allowed others to touch my backpack.

I have always been my biggest critic. I used to recite my failures daily, and not in a healthy "let's reflect and course-correct" kind of way. I lived with regrets and disappointments and wallowed in them. One day, as I was driving home from work and praying about a difficult situation I was facing, I began to apologize once again for all of my mistakes, failures, and short comings.. Tears streamed down my face as God showed me that He had long since forgiven me, but that I had to find a way to let go of those regrets. There was a realization at some point that it didn't make any sense to be my own worst enemy. I stood in the mirror one day, ready to recite my daily affirmation, and I asked myself, "Why would you be enemies with the one person you can control and the one person you can never escape from?"

Unleashing power that was buried inside started with ending the abusive relationship I had with myself. Empowerment came with allowing myself to believe in my ability to do anything I set my mind to. Freedom to grow and become was unhindered when I stopped apologizing for success and rejecting any form of recognition. I took inventory of the words I said to and about myself. Then I started changing my words.

When I was in high school, I noticed how critical I was of other people. To be honest, I fed off of laughter. I *constantly* looked at people around me and compared myself to them. It became an obsessive checklist between how I was doing versus my perception of the world around me. I noticed what other girls wore, more because of insecurity that my family couldn't afford name brands, and less about an interest in fashion. I noticed how popular girls interacted with one another, because I always felt a little on the outside of the crowd due to my Christian faith and my family's low income. Essentially, I never felt like I fit in anywhere. I was too worldly for the Church. I was too "churchy" for the world. I was constantly looking around for my place.

BOND with me here, I still struggle with this. Identity issues have robbed me of progress for a long time. My conservative friends call me liberal, and my liberal friends think I'm conservative. I don't fit into any particular bipartisan box in today's political climate. It has been a lifelong struggle to find a box that I fit comfortably into. People often tell me that I think outside of the box—that's because that's where I have always been. I have never ever fit into a particular viewpoint, group, or stereotype. That makes an insecure person a thousand times more insecure. Not only did I feel awkward, but the world kind of agreed with me.

Even back in high school, I had an internal instinct about changing my thought patterns. I would catch myself being critical or comparing myself to others, then instantly make myself think of three things I liked about that person. I had to dig deep sometimes. That struggle was super-real. I would look across the room at a stranger with crazy makeup, instantly make a "Mimi from Drew Carey" reference, and then once I caught it, force myself to find three positive things about her. Torture. Even worse, I got my friends involved. If I said something mean or judgmental, they made me find three compliments to say out loud. And even worse than that, they used it against me by making me say three positive things about another stranger I often criticized—myself—the girl I saw every day in the mirror, but didn't really know.

I wanted to keep people around me who knew my true character, which was especially hard since I didn't really know myself. Deep down, though, I wanted someone to see past my insecurities and climb the walls I had put up so they could see the real me. And a little piece of me hoped someone else would lovingly tell me who I was, because I was so lost. There are about a hundred reasons why that would never work, but the most important one is that those desires compelled me to become other people's versions of myself, so I was never authentically me. I mimicked a connection with people, and only allowed people to get to know me through a small lens, then I allowed them to dictate my path through their skewed perspective.

The turning point was when I acknowledged that I couldn't go where I was called to go until I was willing to become who I was created to be. That meant ditching old habits that prevented me from thriving and adopting a new belief system rooted in confidence. To change who I was without completely losing myself required that I identify my character, then use that as a foundation to

build upon. Character doesn't change easily, so I knew it
would be the core of who I was.

Chapter Twenty-Four

Humility is Not Insecurity

I wanted to anchor myself to the positive attributes I possessed, like honesty, kindness, integrity, and loyalty. Identifying positive qualities in myself proved to be another huge hurdle for me. One of my heroes in life was my paternal grandmother. She had very strong views about humility. I remember her correcting strangers because she didn't want them to tell me I was pretty out of fear that it would "go to my head." She had zero tolerance for bragging. She held fast to the belief that too many compliments would incite pride, and pride set people up to fall. Because of my deep love for my Mema, it took me a long time to admit that not all of my beliefs aligned with hers, and that was okay. But once I differentiated loyalty from blind agreement, I was able to establish my own world views.

When I revisited beliefs that fostered insecurity and self-doubt in the name of humility, I realized how flawed my thinking was. I mislabeled insecurity as humility. They are not the same, not even close. Humility entails respect for other people as humans, filled with wisdom of their own, beliefs of their own, and much to offer the world. Humility by definition is about modesty and respect.

By definition, humility is when I have a low view of my own importance, acknowledging that others around me may be smarter, wiser, or more skilled than I am, but instead of being threatened by them, I value and learn from them. Humility creates mentors and heroes. With humility, I can honor someone as the individual they are, with their own points of view, even when our views are different. Humility listens and creates space for diversity.

In contrast, insecurity happens when I constantly compare myself to the world around me from the vantage point of inadequacy. Instead of a low view of my importance or position, insecurity is a low view of myself as an individual. Insecurity is defined as uncertainty or anxiety about oneself, a lack of confidence. Insecurity is what causes me to justify and defend my own existence and world views. It compels me to attack others, lash out, get jealous, or self-destruct in silence in reaction to the threats from the world around me and the people in it. Insecurity breeds intolerance. Insecurity shows up as harsh or knee-jerk reactions when I don't feel others are listening to me or valuing my views. Particularly, when I am insecure, my personal value is directly linked to how others value me. So while humility creates heroes and mentors, insecurity creates rivals.

Where I placed my self-worth made a real impact in shifting my trajectory and guiding me to peace. Insecurity caused me to doubt who God said I am, and how He saw me as His personal creation. God sees my heart and my nature through His Daddy eyes of love. He sees me as a person, not a performance. He has the ability to look past the walls I put up. He saw who I really was, and He told me who I am. Becoming His version of myself enabled me to become the person I had always dreamed of being.

As I transformed and gained confidence as divinely empowered woman, others noticed. I started getting requests to help others, and I wanted to help them all! I excelled at adapting and overcoming obstacles. I powered through to complete projects others had quit or failed.

One time when I was working at a high school, I was approached by one of the assistant principals to put together a last-minute Senior Show, an annual end-of-the-year tradition that showcased the talent of the graduating seniors. For some reason, the show was falling apart, the sponsors had backed out, and I had three weeks to find talent and pull it all off. The principal knew exactly what it would take for me to say *yes*, "Andi, if anyone can do this, it's you." I didn't ask questions. I grabbed my cape and went into save-the-day mode.

I wasn't told that I wouldn't have ANY rehearsal time on the stage at all because the band was preparing for a competition. The day the students performed in front of their classmates was the first time they'd been on mic. I took every obstacle in stride, and we powered through. I arrived in the auditorium two hours before the show to find that the stage was still completely filled with instruments. We were scrambling to clear the stage, including mopping up actual spit from the floor where students had emptied their spit valves onto the stage. It was gross.

To make matters worse, the administration had a time schedule to adhere to. So they brought the senior class down at the scheduled time, but the sound system was not yet set up or working properly. The teacher responsible for the sound just shrugged and said they didn't know why it wasn't working and left. True story, they actually left and went back to their classroom, leaving me with a gym full of rowdy seniors, one working microphone, and no idea how to fix any of it. We had to go live with the one working mic and really horrible sound. The MC's jokes failed, their minute-to-win-it games flopped, a few disorderly students completely tried to hijack the show for their moment in the spotlight. It was a *disaster*. We seriously considered cutting our losses and cancelling the major performance scheduled for that evening.

Then, something magical happened. The Associate Principal brought in the district audio/visual expert who fixed our sound system and worked with our students to get them ready for their evening performance in front of their parents. They fixed the sound system and got us ready to go. I ordered pizzas for all of my students and asked them to stay after school to get the show together. They performed that night in front of classmates and parents, and it was incredible. It was a completely different show. With the right tools at work, everything else fell into place.

I have always worked well in the midst of the chaos life threw my way, which in some cases, can be a great skill. However, because we were designed to adapt, chaos became a way of life for me. It's how I functioned best. I could get into crisis mode quickly, living life reactively instead of taking control. One of my mentors told me, "It is almost impossible to live out your calling in reaction to life. Success is intentional. The pathway to your purpose is filled with tiny deliberate steps that take you to your goal." I had adapted plans, adjusted expectations, revised goals, and compromised my whole life.

As an adult in the workforce, I was every boss' dream employee. I adopted the plan and made it happen. For me, Plan B was to go back and make Plan A work. I always found a way to make it happen. It might look at little different than I had envisioned, but I'd pull it off at the cost of my own physical or emotional well-being. I had zero self-preservation instincts. So even though I was succeeding in making other people's life easier, as a human trying to function in life with a shred of peace and happiness, I was failing.

When I first started this journey, I came to realize how restless I was. If I wasn't in a crisis, I was preparing for a crisis. The biggest problem with that is that I didn't allow myself to dream because I was always reacting to what was happening in the moment. I stopped making long-term plans. I could form short-term plans to reach a goal, but not know what do once I got there. For instance, I knew how to lose weight, but not how to live a healthy lifestyle. I knew how to build my business, but not how to run it.

It was shocking to learn that my reactions were connected to broken foundations. I had to go back and figure out where some of my distorted views came from so I could root them out and replace them with healthier ones. I had to change my connotation with words like *sex, love, forgiveness, father,* and *family.* I had to identify the flaws in my faith that were preventing me from letting go of old thought patterns.

I played softball growing up. It was one of my favorite sports because I came from a baseball family. When I was learning to throw the ball, my grandfather taught me that the ball would go where my feet were pointing. When I missed the mark from where I thought I was aiming, I had to go back and adjust my feet to make sure they were planted in the right place and pointed in right direction. That same concept worked in the battle of my mind. My thoughts were controlling my trajectory, and in order to get where I was trying to go, I had to bring my thoughts into alignment with my destiny. If my path was off, I had to go back to the foundation and check where my feet were pointing.

God cares about my thoughts because thoughts drive destiny. The Bible says that as a man thinketh, so is he. (Proverbs 23:7 KJV) It says in Romans 12:2 and Ephesians 4:22-24 that we are to be transformed by the renewal of our minds. Philippians 4:8 tells us that we are to train our minds to think on things that are honorable, just, pure, lovely, commendable, of excellence and worthy of praise. Isaiah 26:3 says that He will keep in **perfect peace** those whose minds are stayed on Him. 2 Corinthians 10:5 tells us to take every thought captive to obey Christ. The Bible is clear about the power of our mind and its ability to direct our path.

When I focused my thoughts on my goals, I made progress. However, when I allowed my thoughts to zero in on my insecurities, doubts, and problems, I experienced setbacks. I didn't really trust myself. I would secure a goal, then quit. I constantly wanted to see what other people were doing and how they did it. I read every book I could find on becoming successful. Then, I would identify a problem area in my life and set out on a mission to fix it by mirroring what I saw other people do. I was always looking for someone else to tell me the way, to empower me to do something great. I formed my plans from what seemed to be working for other people, instead of daring to live out the dream God had called me to.

I hated making decisions, like to a ridiculous extreme. I hated going to restaurants because menus were completely overwhelming, too many choices without very much information. I lived in a "you get what you get" mindset and didn't acknowledge that I had the right to ask or choose for myself. I found myself constantly looking at reviews before I bought anything, trusting complete strangers to help me make decisions, so that I could minimize the risk of being wrong or failing.

I wanted to move out of reaction mode, crisis mode, and even overcomer mode. I wanted to operate from a place of intentional living. Intentional living involves planning, reflecting, course-correcting, and action. It is fluid, ever-changing, as I learn and grow. There is an old Chinese Proverb that says:

> *Be careful of your thoughts,*
> *for your thoughts become your words.*
> *Be careful of your words,*
> *for your words become your actions.*
> *Be careful of your actions,*
> *for your actions become your habits.*
> *Be careful of your habits,*
> *for your habits become your character.*
> *Be careful of your character,*
> *for your character becomes your destiny.*

If I wanted to change my destiny, I had to change my habits, which meant that I had to change my actions, which meant that I had to change my words, which meant that I had to change my thoughts. I was in my own way. My mind was the roadblock to my destiny. My thoughts would pave or destroy the path to my destiny. The real truth to becoming an empowered woman, all depended on me getting out of my own mind.

Chapter Twenty-Five

The Bank Account Principal

After working through forgiveness, identity, and self-worth, I had one more major obstacle to overcome before I could experience total mental, emotional, and spiritual freedom. I had to repair the cracks in my foundation about love and relationships. Separating my sexual identity from my self-worth felt like emotional surgery. Throughout the recovery process, I was able to clearly see that I didn't have a healthy image of Christ-like love. Nor did I understand His plan for relationships. But once I understood the Bank Account Principal, I was able to navigate relationships and communicate more effectively.

Essentially, The Bank Account Principal theorizes that we all come into relationships with negative or positive equity based on our past experiences. This is true, regardless of the type of relationship. Past experiences which broke trust, abused power, violated unity, or failed to fulfill needs equate to negative equity. Past experiences which established strong connections, embraced freedom, celebrated individuality, and offered healthy support of the other party build positive equity.

I began to build relationships with The Bank Account Principal in mind. I navigated conversations better and established better boundaries because I understood that people came into my life with positive or negative equity. Every action and conversation we had either made a deposit or withdrawal into our new relationship account.

Depending on the effort we both invested into the friendship, we either built a nice nest egg that would sustain a long-term relationship, or we set ourselves up for bankruptcy.

I discovered that deposits were made into the account through thoughtful deeds, random acts of kindness, compliments, honesty, respect, trust, appreciating the other person's interests, respecting boundaries, offering support, creating memories, or laughing together. In contrast, if either of us did something that was entirely selfish in nature, outside of our integrity (one of my favorite Brené Brown phrases), cruel, angry, dishonest, or thoughtless, it would make a withdrawal from our relationship account.

BOND with me here. It may seem unfair, but we don't get to decide the quantities of deposits or withdrawals. Quantities are established based on love languages and connotation triggers. It's not a brownie point system. I have had numerous relationships that fell apart because we stopped making deposits into our account and allowed those resources to be depleted when our time and attention were spent elsewhere.

The Five Love Languages by Gary Chapman helped me communicate love more effectively. Not only did it help me understand my own love language, but it also taught me how to communicate love in way that it was received well by the people closest to me, especially my son. Before I understood the love languages, I used to make the mistake of assuming I should give the other person what I was looking for, not recognizing that I may be working extremely hard, yet leaving their needs unfulfilled. For example, my love language is words of affirmation. Compliments work for me but paying compliments to someone who craves quality time doesn't meet their long-term need of feeling love in the way that is true to them. Once I learned to look beyond myself, my wants, my desires, and my needs, I was able to see the needs of others more clearly. When I expressed my needs effectively from a place of communication, rather than manipulation, I was much more fulfilled in relationships. Once I began to focus on the deposits I made into a relationship, becoming a contributor, not just a consumer, I had healthier, longer lasting relationships.

One of the key components for me was learning that my needs were my responsibility. It was not realistic to ask one person to meet all of my spiritual, emotional, mental, physical, and sexual needs. I created codependent relationships and put my partners in impossible situations because I wanted to be their everything and wanted them to be mine. While I was usually consistent in making deposits into the relationship account, I would have emotional melt downs that violated trust and equated to huge withdrawals.

Trauma, emotional insecurity, broken self-image, distorted sexual identity, uncertainty, times when I felt rushed, and extremely negative experiences in relationships all became my emotional and spiritual battle scars, disfiguring my self-worth. I rebounded from relationship to relationship before my wounds could heal, entering the next one with negative emotional equity and a severely overdrawn relationship account before a new relationship could even begin.

I often allowed people into the spaces of my heart and mind who had no intentions of staying. I blurred the lines between intentions and actions and lost sight of what it meant to truly love and be loved. I had grown up with the mindset that I'd be married by eighteen, a concept that stemmed from expectations spoken over me. My biological father's side of the family made frequent remarks about me being married by the time I was eighteen. I accepted that as my fate for a long time, and when I didn't get married at eighteen, I struggled to figure out what was wrong with me. I built my identity on who I would be to my future husband. I became what I thought he would want me to be, which meant I had established my entire identity and self-worth on preconceived notions and stereotypes about what I thought men wanted.

In a quest to understand God's version of love, I determined that I wanted to be someone who loves on purpose. I didn't want to offer emotionally driven sentiments, but rather make commitments to the people closest to me that "I will love you unconditionally, and I will do it on purpose." I understood more than anyone that half of all marriages fail. *For the record 100% of my marriages have failed.* For a long time, I determined that I just wasn't wife material. In truth, it wasn't so much that I wasn't wife material, as much as it was that I got married for the wrong reasons...twice. Different wrong reasons each time, but wrong reasons none the less. Even beyond romantic relationships, if I look at the friendships I have lost over the years, I have to admit that I made emotionally driven decisions based on connection and hope.

Since I tied my value to how others valued me, my relationships were unstable. I embraced a distorted concept of what others wanted from me. I was wrong, and I unjustly projected my fears onto good people who didn't deserve to carry my baggage. I pushed away people who challenged my skewed views and kept people around who reinforced them. I was a dive-in-head-first and deal-with-the-consequences-later kind of girl. As a result, I picked up the pieces of my broken heart time and time again. Each time, I lost a piece of who I was, and the wall around my heart was reinforced.

I saw the most damaging effects in my dating relationships. When I did finally commit, I was smothering and needy. If my significant other was having a bad day, I took it as personal rejection that I didn't make him happy. If my partner wasn't happy, I had failed him. If he wasn't in the mood for sex, I perceived it as personal rejection, obviously he wasn't attracted to me. I was a wreck. It was absolutely as exhausting as it sounds...for both of us. Here is the flip side of that. I loved deeply, was forgiving, and unconditionally supportive. While I had a warped perception of love, I did love 1,000%, all-in, from day one, to the very best of my ability.

CHAPTER TWENTY-SIX

Unconditional Love Is...

My inability to understand true love impacted me in every area. I particularly struggled in church. It was difficult for me to accept love from God because I didn't feel like I deserved His love. I didn't know what I could do to make God *want* to love me or keep loving me. I was completely lost. As someone who constantly compared myself to others, I struggled in church. I took mental snapshots of friends, acquaintances, and happy couples, and based my entire opinion of who I should be on those brief moments of time. I saw those people for two hours every Sunday, literally 1% of their week, and determined their whole narrative in my mind based on 1% of their time.

I had huge doubts about faith. I didn't understand God, and I especially didn't understand His people, so how could I be saved? I could never earn the type of love that sacrificed the way Jesus did. I knew there was no act in the world great enough to earn the love that was demonstrated by a parent giving their child's life to save mine the way God did. Somewhere in the mix, I realized that God's love wasn't on the auction block. He wasn't offering it to highest bidder or giving it away as a prize for the best works in the church. He was offering me love beyond anything I had ever known, and He was giving it to me freely. God didn't want anything *from* me. He wanted *me*.

I spent a lot of time shattered for the first forty years of my life. God would fix my broken heart and send me on my way, as any perfect Dad would do. Yet, I'd always manage to break it again. After my second divorce, when God was picking up the pieces of my broken heart once more, I gave up hope of ever finding love, and I accepted that I was a complete and total failure, unworthy of receiving love. God began to reveal His version of love to me. He spelled it out in 1 Corinthians 13, giving me a checklist of what to look for when answering the question, "Do they love me?" *because God knew I would need a checklist.* In His divine checklist in 1 Corinthians, I have a gauge that tells me exactly what love is, so there is no question as to how I am supposed to treat people or be treated by people.

Love is patient, love is kind. It does not envy, it does not boast, it is not proud. It does not dishonor others, it is not self-seeking, it is not easily angered, it keeps no record of wrongs. Love does not delight in evil but rejoices with the truth. It always protects, always trusts, always hopes, always perseveres. Love never fails.

1 John 4:7 says that God *is* love. Not just that God loves us, but that He *is* love. As I was searching to find out who God was as a Person, and to learn about His character, I found the answers in 1 Corinthians 13. God *is* love. He is patient, He is kind, He does not envy, He does not boast, He is not proud, He does not dishonor others, He is not self-seeking, He is not easily angered, He keeps no record of wrongs, He does not delight in evil, He rejoices with the truth, He always protects, always trusts, always hopes, always perseveres and never fails.

I began to truly get that down in my spirit, how God *is* love to His very core. To take it a step further, I began to understand that this is how God wants me to love people and how they are supposed to love me back. When I prayed the prayer, "God make my heart mirror Yours," I was asking God to make me more like Love. I could stop questioning feelings and whether or not someone truly loved me. I now had a brilliant checklist in 1 Corinthians to let me know where I stood with people. God knew that I would need more information. He knew my finite mind couldn't fathom perfect love. He knew that I would stray far from His plan for loving relationships, so He gave me a guidepost.

One of my favorite quotes of all time came from Steve Harvey, who told a young lady on his radio show to stop believing what people tell her just because it's what she wanted to hear. I was completely guilty of that. I would ignore what people did as long as they said the right things. It took me a very long time to understand how meaningless words are without actions behind them.

If I told someone I unconditionally loved them, then I was committing to be unconditionally patient with them. When I began to act or react impatiently, then I was acting outside of the love commitment that I made. I knew I would fall short and miss the mark sometimes, however I established a strategy to acknowledge my shortcomings quickly, apologize, and correct. If I truly loved someone, they were worthy of my time, understanding, and patience, unconditionally. Even when they were running late, even when they drove me crazy, and even when they made the same mistakes repeatedly. Unconditionally. It would have been silly to stop loving others when they made mistakes, so why did I feel it was okay for others to love me without patience? Patience became a key indicator of how someone truly felt about me, or how I felt about them. It was an accurate barometer because when our relationship was not aligned, impatience was usually the first sign to surface.

Unconditional love also involves unconditional kindness. I view kindness as thoughtful actions that are selfless in nature. Cruelty and abuse are the opposite of love because love is always kind. I look back at the abusive cycles of my toxic relationships. My partners would cross boundaries, and I would threaten to leave. They would convince me that they loved me and promise that whatever had happened would never happen again, so I would stay. The cycle was the same, whether it was getting up in my face screaming at me and calling me names, or addiction binges, or cheating, or lying. I held on, thinking I could love them through it. I convinced myself that they loved me. I think I might have made different decisions if I had stopped and asked myself if they were being kind to me instead of justifying or enabling their behavior.

Loving unconditionally means that I am unconditionally celebrating the other person and not allowing myself to become envious of their success, happiness, where they spend their time, or with whom they spend it. That's tough, but it's tied to unconditional trust and unconditional hope. It's also tied to unconditionally not keeping a record of wrongs. When we love people, we aren't comparing ourselves to them, nor are we comparing them to other people. Love doesn't try to make another person measure up to our idealistic views. I think sometimes I have erred on the extreme when it comes to unconditional trust, hope, and keeping no record of wrongs. God did not call us to put ourselves in dangerous or abusive situations. I learned to set better boundaries that came from a place of respect and integrity without the intent to control or manipulate. The unconditional trust component doesn't mean that I have to allow people to hurt me time and time again.

Love protects, and it does not dishonor the other person. There is a soap-opera-worthy version of love that is self-seeking. Its mantra is, "Look out for #1." The idea that love should be self-seeking is false. Love uplifts the other person and brings honor to them. Love protects them, not just physically to keep them from harm, but love protects their heart and their mind, too. Love protects their reputation and doesn't say harmful things to or about them. Love is fierce. Love is safe...unconditionally.

What would happen in my relationships if I stopped accepting less and started demanding real love from people who were going to hold a place of influence in my life? What if I upped the price on the value of my heart, instead of just giving it away to the highest bidder? I think those two questions were the catalyst for my period of being intentionally single. Taking a step back from "love" enabled me to expand my views on love outside of romance and establish better love habits.

The Godly definition of love goes against everything society tells me that love is all about. I think it even goes against some of my natural self-preservation instincts. For a long time, I thought the 1 Corinthians kind of love was idealistic and unattainable. I don't think we, in and of ourselves, can be, or should even try to be, perfect. To me, it's about setting a standard to strive for to be patient and kind with the people we love in our lives. It's an intentional effort to give the benefit of the doubt to those we love, and to truly forgive and move on if we say we are going to forgive them. There will be times that envy creeps in, that jealousy rears its head, or that fear tries to wedge its way back in. The best tool in my arsenal to combat a threat to love is open and honest dialogue.

CHAPTER TWENTY-SEVEN

We Weren't Made to Do This Alone

My tribe is comprised of fierce women and strong men who have my back no matter what. I am honored that they trust me to partner with them in life. When I share struggles with them, they build me up. When I confide in them, I don't have to worry about that information being used against me or being the source of gossip when I'm not around. I love our coffee dates or sitting down for a glass of wine on a patio with them, because I leave feeling energized and refreshed, and I hope they do too.

Loving was never the hard part for me. I struggled with allowing other people to get close enough to love me back. I had a terrible habit of telling people something that sounded deep, but that did not reveal anything that might come back to harm me if it got out. It was difficult to step outside of my "include everyone" mantra and realize that I have the right to choose my inner circle. It would be better to do life alone than to do life with people who don't truly care about me.

I had always heard that friends were there for you when you were down, but sometimes the people who were there for me didn't have the right motives. I have since learned that even more than being there for me during the hard times, true friends celebrate the wins too, and encourage me to press forward. With real friends, I don't have to apologize for success; I don't have to downplay excitement; and I don't have to choose between our friendship and my career. My tribe doesn't try to control me or force me to fit into their own limitations.

In the past, because I wore my scars like badges of honor, and I was openly desperate for connection and comradery. I made myself an easy target for people who would use me. I was drawn to people whom I believed would protect me, not realizing that what I needed were people who would be a silent strength while I protected myself. I didn't need people to fix my brokenness; I needed them to be there with me while I fixed it myself. Breaking the cycle of codependency gave me the freedom I needed to connect with people without fear of abandonment. I didn't have to fear friends walking out of my life when my life was no longer dependent upon their presence in it. My friends enrich my life, they don't define it.

Something that caught me off guard as I continued to get stronger was how much I needed other strong women in my life. I needed to bond with women and form beautiful friendships that I hadn't experienced before. For decades, I didn't really see what I had to offer my female friends. I nurtured my scars from past insults and allowed my pain to eclipse the shining stars who gave me strength and courage even in childhood.

It was easier to remember the lessons I learned through pain, like the insecurity that started in the second grade with a group of girls who made fun of me because I walked differently than they did. It was my first experience with body shame. I didn't know how to shrug off their snide remarks back then, nor did I know how to explain that I was not a small girl like they were. I had a big booty, and big booties look differently when they walk than skinny booties. Instead of knowing what to say, I just silently absorbed the sting of their comments. The lie I wanted to believe was that all girls were mean and that none of them would ever accept me. Then I met Madison Antweil that same year, and she would become my first real friend. In fact, she is still one of the people I feel most connected to. We have a mutually honest and vulnerable relationship. She is one of my "sheroes" and one of the fiercest members of my tribe. When I moved away from that school in sixth grade, it was Madison that I missed most. While I made new friends, and for a few years Madison I lost touch, *mostly because were twelve,* we would reconnect later in life and pick up where we left off on the school playground.

It would be easy to relive the betrayal I felt when I showed up to the first day of the seventh grade and every single one of my sixth-grade friends had decided together that they wanted nothing to do with me anymore. I had a complete melt down after my first day of Junior High. I'm pretty sure I wailed out some teenage drama version of, "I'm never going to school again." However, refusing to completely close off to the world, I met some really cool people that year. Through friendships that are almost three decades long, I had to rethink my theory about all friends leaving eventually. My friends Amanda, Dawn, and Cynthia are still an important part of my life.

I could have held onto the sting of rejection I felt when some of the people in my youth group decided I was "too churchy" to hang around with. I could have accepted the lie that I didn't have a place and that nobody would ever want me around. However, I did life with some really amazing mentors and friends with whom I truly connected, even after that rejection. Some of my closest friendships with people like Glynda, Debbie, Ruby, Nacole, Jessica, and Kevin are still going strong. I don't even remember some of the names of the people who didn't want me around because the pain wasn't as important as the people who took the time to earn space in my heart.

Long lasting, mutual friendships were not natural for me. My friendships with all of these people evolved over time. There were seasons that we were close and connected, and then we'd go weeks, months, or even years without talking. However, when we would reconnect, it would be like no time had passed at all.

Throughout my adult life, I had to work hard to not isolate myself. The lies I believed about friendships crept back in like weeds that hadn't been pulled out by the root. However, when I lived in East Texas and got really sick, a team surrounded me and helped me through a ninety-six-day migraine and all of the crises that came before and after. Rachelle, Lori, Diana, Linda, and Amy all took me to the hospital at different times, seeing me at my absolute worst and asking nothing in return. Angie, Jessica, Christina and Dean rallied around me, wore *Team Andi* shirts, and checked on me every single day. I was devastated to move away from them when I came back to Dallas/Fort Worth to recover. I thought I was leaving them behind, but then I learned about friendship beyond distance. I didn't have a new circle, my circle just expanded. I added Danielle, Sophia, Sarah, Carey Jo, Will, Julie, and Ashley.

As my circle got bigger and bigger, I began to have hope in people again. I stopped telling myself that I was alone. I stopped isolating myself as much. I reached out when I needed a friend, and I learned to have mutually open and honest friendships with people who loved me for who I am. I also began to embrace a friendship with my mom and my sisters Elicia, Kim, and my sister-in-love Heather.

I had grown weary of doing life alone in the name of independence. I was tired of saying *no* to coffee dates or being too afraid of rejection to ask a friend to have lunch. One of the first people I met up with on a regular basis was Andria Flores, who is now my editor. Andria and I connected on life philosophies and core beliefs. We have similar parenting techniques and similar philosophies on emotional and spiritual healing. We also connect on fundamental spiritual beliefs. We quickly established open and honest dialogue with healthy boundaries. That was exactly what I had been looking for! I needed that.

I have had some great male friends in my life, men whom I could call today and they'd be there for me if I needed them. However, I found myself at a time in life that I needed relationships with women who could relate to my daily struggles. I needed people who knew what it was like to cry at 7 AM for absolutely no reason at all. I needed to bond with someone who understood that we could be standing outside in twenty-degree weather, and out of some sort of hormonal sorcery only women know, I'd have a hot flash. I needed to bond with people who knew what it was like to love your kids intensely, but also want nothing more in life than to take a long hot shower alone without anyone knocking on the door for fifteen minutes.

I needed women in my life who had overcome trauma and understood what it was like to rebuild their mind from the ground up. I needed fierce, strong mentors who were brave enough to ask for help when they needed it, courageous enough to be honest even in their brokenness, and spiritually solid enough to join me in prayer when I faced a battle. I needed friends who meant it when they said, "I'm praying for you." I needed women who would call me out on my mess and were equally candid to reach out in love when they saw me self-destructing. I needed those friends, and I needed to *be* that friend. As much as I needed them in my life, I desperately needed the fulfillment of being in theirs too.

I have come to value myself and internalize that I am worthy of friendships with both men and women because of the person that I am, not what I can do for them. Maybe one of the most fulfilling emotions I have experienced is feeling accepted by someone who wants nothing from me except my presence because I bring joy to their life.

I received a kind note one day that read, "I hope one day you see that people love you for who you are, not what you do for them." I will forever remember those words from my dear friend Vaughna Kromann, whose mama-heart is connected to mine forever because of her precious daughter Ashley, whom she allowed me to mentor.

My support team is built upon the concept that real friends do not control me, manipulate me, or enable me. In my healthy friendships, I am accepted for who I am, encouraged to grow, and held accountable. BOND with me here. I had to learn the importance of my tribe and how their habits impacted mine. I could not become who I wanted to be if I continued to surround myself with people who acted the way I used to act and did things I didn't want to do anymore. I had to step away from people I cared about, but who were toxic to me.

When I began developing healthy boundaries, not all of my friends celebrated that with me. Some of them could not handle the shift in my priorities. Some didn't want to talk as much once I quit gossiping with them. I wasn't as much fun to complain to once I refrained from joining in the rant. I didn't go on an excommunication spree and cut everyone out of my life at the same time. Toxic people had a tendency to remove themselves once I stopped being toxic with them. Users stopped hanging around when I stopped allowing myself to be used. Part time friends quit coming around when I began offering them the same level of investment that they offered me.

When it comes friendship, my son is my hero. Country would rather have no friends at all, than to have bad friends around him. He has always guarded his inner circle. I have heard him sit down and have a heart-to-heart conversation with one of his football brothers to tell him that he loved him and would always be a phone call away, but until the young man stopped smoking marijuana, he had to keep his distance. I have seen him end a friendship because the other person didn't value right and wrong in the way he did. He went to a friend's house one time and took a huge step back in the friendship after witnessing how disrespectful the kid was to his parents. He chose to stay away from anyone who was drinking or using drugs. He didn't compromise his integrity for anyone. I admire that. Country was respected among his peers because of his integrity. His circle is solid now, filled with other young men of integrity who share his values—and his intense passion for video games.

As seasons change, the role someone plays in my life often shifts, too. I have noticed this happens when people move away, get married, have a baby, or start a new career. Our genuine love for each other remains, but our role in each other's life is often altered by the impact of the twists and turns in our individual paths. The amount of time we spend together may decrease in response to new responsibilities and demands. I learned to accept people where they are and stopped trying to pull more out of a friendship than what the other person is willing to or able to offer. I started allowing friendships to take their own shape without predefined expectations. The result has been lasting friendships that are fluid and uniquely and totally our own.

I am careful who I allow into my inner circle. The people closest to me are the ones I share my secrets with. I share my dreams and hopes without fear of judgment. When I started my self-improvement plan, I didn't tell many people because I didn't feel that I could deal with people's advice at the time. I have learned that what I say publicly will be commented on publicly. What I choose to share freely, people feel free to advise me on. I can share raw information with my inner circle that I would only present publicly after it has been refined and polished through research, reflection, and a solid plan of action.

When I began selecting mentors and asking them to invest their time in me, I approached them with the confidence that I am worthy of asking. I made a list of qualities and knowledge that I needed to get where I wanted to go, and next to those qualities, I wrote the name of someone I knew or wanted to know who had the knowledge or embodied the quality I sought. I started with the person who appeared most often on my list and asked them for an hour of their time once a month.

I chose mentors who would partner with me, teach me, and offer me encouragement. I avoided relationships where the other person just told me what to do or did it for me. I also avoided acquiring mentors who would try to fight my battles for me. I don't think I could have made it this far in life without my older sister Elicia or my mom.

My older sister has stood beside me in the Customer Service line while I had panic attacks returning clothes that didn't fit. She has answered the phone to the sound of my cries because I couldn't complete a menial task in public, like going into a crowded restaurant to place a large order of food. She has sent food back for me when the order was wrong, and I was too embarrassed to speak up. I think she is ten times stronger than I am and so much more comfortable in her own skin. Her strength and confidence make her the perfect ally. She has always been skilled to know when to push me to do something and when to rescue me because I truly wasn't ready for the task at hand.

My mom is another defender. She has a way of getting things done eloquently, but still making it very clear that she is not playing around. I could tell a million stories about times she interceded on my behalf when I was growing up: the times she'd show up at the school, fully put together and calm on the surface, but inside she was fierce and ready to fight. One time my sixth-grade teacher decided I was lying about a wrist sprain and made me take off the Ace bandage that my mom had wrapped it with. I believe it was Mom's question, "Are you prepared to take on medical liability for my child?" that got the principal's attention.

It wasn't just when I was a kid. During my second marriage, our whole family was planning to go out to eat. I was sick, and even though my husband wanted to go to Six Flags, I wasn't up for it. He was furious. While my family went to their cars so they could head to the restaurant, we stayed behind for a minute so he could "talk" to me. He didn't realize that my brother had come back in the house when he started screaming at me and calling me names. I, of course, cried, which only made matters worse. Neither of us knew that my brother was outside of the bedroom door making the decision on whether to come in and handle the situation or to go get my mom. He chose to get my mom. I have never seen her as fierce as when she came through the bedroom door. I don't remember all of her words, but I do remember that she made it clear he had crossed a line. She looked him in the eyes and told him that she wasn't scared of him. *I was.* He stormed across the room toward her, but she stepped toward him, fearless. Not only was she in mama bear mode, but she also knew my dad was nearby, and he'd never let anything happen to us. I needed a defender in that moment because I wasn't at a place in my life yet that I could defend myself.

There was a time relatively recently that I was having a hard time getting my car back from a body shop. Mom picked me up and said we were going to see about my car. I thought one thing: *Oh, no.* I had not been able to get a straight answer from them, and I was out-of-pocket for a rental that I had been driving for over a month. When we arrived at the body shop and the adjuster started talking in circles again, I quickly got rattled, but Mom didn't. I wish I could have recorded the look on the man's face when he started lying to me and mom said in the most calm, yet assertive, tone, "I assume you always have terrible service, and this has nothing to do with her being a single, female customer." She has never been afraid to call out a truth and expose wrongdoing. She gets action when it seems like nobody else can.

There have been times, like those, when I needed a defender. I needed the solidarity of my tribe. I needed the person who was trying to cause me harm to know that I was not alone. With support, I became more courageous.

Every goal I achieved, even the small ones, boosted my confidence and relaxed insecurity's grip on me. Every battle I fought with my team's support silenced anxiety just a little more. Every time I made myself do something that had previously paralyzed me, I grew stronger. I was able to confront issues in my past, tell my story, break bad habits, eat in restaurants alone, and eventually, free myself to dream again. Conquering each source of anxiety one by one, I finally unpacked a backpack of weight that I had lugged around for years.

When God gave me the dream for my ministry, I felt a nervous excitement about the seed that had been planted inside of me. I could only compare it to what I experienced when I was pregnant with Country. As he grew inside of me, I studied parenting and child development. I searched the internet to find out what part of his body was developing each day, and I prayed over that body system. As he grew, my tummy stretched, and my body changed. There were unpleasant symptoms like morning sickness, aching muscles and joints, weight gain, cravings, and mood swings. The more miserable I became, the more ready I was for him to get here.

I went into labor at 25 weeks, but luckily, they were able to stop it. The nurse explained that babies who are born at twenty-five weeks have many complications and that I needed to keep him in as long as possible. They hydrated me and made me rest, and I would go on to carry him full-term. As I prepared for him, my mom and I went to garage sales every weekend. I stocked up on clothes and supplies. I readied his room. I prepared for him. As the end drew near, I began to have Braxton Hicks contractions, which were like a fire drill for my body to practice what would happen when I actually went into labor. My stomach stretched beyond what I thought was humanly possible. The ligaments that supported the weight of my baby were stretched. My hip dislocated as my pelvis spread to prepare for birth. There were changes happening in my body daily.

I fell in love with my son, playing with him before I even gave birth to him. I laid in bed at night, and I'd poke a part of my tummy, and he'd kick my finger. Then, I'd poke another part, and he'd hit that one. I watched in awe as he moved around in my belly. I even have a picture in which you can clearly see his arm imprint through my shirt. By the time February came, I was ready. I was excited to meet him. He had finished developing, and it was time for him to make his appearance in the world.

Our dreams are like a pregnancy. They begin with an idea, a seed, that we have to nurture and foster. As we lay the groundwork for our dream to manifest, we grow more and more excited and ready. It can be hard to focus on where we are because we want to experience where we are going. False labor can throw us off. It looks like the real thing, but it's just not time yet. Prematurely launching a dream can have negative consequences, just like having a premature baby can cause complications. As the fruition of the dream draws closer, we get more and more uncomfortable and experience greater anticipation for what lies ahead.

The message God gave me when I started was, "Wait. Hold steady. Don't launch prematurely."

I always end my radio show with action items and final thoughts, and I want to do same here. As I am writing this message, I feel a sense of pride that is foreign to me. I finally did what I set out to do more than twenty years ago. I pray that you have benefitted from this journey with me, and that you have found key action items to apply to your own life. I pray that you have discovered that you are not alone in your journey.

When you shed negative emotions that once prevented you from moving forward toward your calling, I hope you experience the presence of God in a new way. For me, that freedom allowed me to have an enriched prayer life, and I began to hear God's voice again. I was able to experience His healing presence without my former feelings of unworthiness. I eventually started dreaming and getting prophetic words again, a spiritual gift that had grown silent in my life for years.

When I was a little girl, I dreamed of my grandparents' car accident about two weeks before it happened. I was terrified that if I told anyone about my dream, then the nightmare would come true. Several years after the wreck, I finally shared the dream with my mom, and there were specific details that I had seen in my dream that I had no other way of knowing, except that God showed them to me, preparing my heart for what was ahead.

In my early thirties, I was attending a small church in Athens, Texas. I received words of encouragement for others in the congregation. When I would hear God speak, I would write down the message as quickly as I could and slip it to the person discretely. One time, right after I started visiting the church, I felt like I was supposed to tell a woman that God saw her tears. I didn't know her, but when I gave her the note out of obedience, she knew exactly what it meant. Another time the message was to simply tell a woman that she was beautiful and perfectly made the way she was by her Creator. When I said those words, she cried deep, sorrowful tears as God began to heal her wounded heart. She had battled her self-image and carried deep wounds caused by the thoughtless words, "You would be gorgeous if you would just lose weight." I was honored that God used me to tell her that He looked at her and saw *beautiful.*

The most terrifying time God used me to give a word to someone happened during another church service. We had a guest speaker for a revival service and many were gathered around the altar in prayer. The worship played quietly, and many people were being healed emotionally across the room. I was standing near the front of the church where a large group of people were praying. I could feel the Holy Spirit moving throughout the congregation. Then I felt God nudge me to write a message for the guest speaker's wife, who was sitting in front of me. I physically looked up at the ceiling, thinking, *Now? Can't I tell her after the service?* He didn't answer me. I am actually pretty sure He rolled His eyes.

I wrote out the message as quickly as I could and slid it into her hand before I lost the courage to obey God. I tried to move back to my seat before she saw me. However, as a plus size woman trying to maneuver the narrow distance between seat aisles, let's just say my stealthy ninja skills failed me. She read the message and began to wail. I'm talking about, shut-the-whole-service-down, I-broke-her, kind of wailing. Tears streamed down my face. I thought, *what in the world have I done?* Guilt and shame burned inside of me, and I wanted to disappear. Obviously, I had missed the message. She went to the stage where her husband still stood holding the microphone, the slightly crumpled note was held tightly in her hand, damp with tears. Without speaking a word or explaining why, she took the microphone from her husband and pointed at me.

"That woman doesn't know me," she began.

I stood as still as possible, as if somehow not moving would cause me to disappear.

She continued, "That woman of God, she doesn't know me, or my family."

Embarrassed, tears scalded my face. I silently apologized to God.

"She has never met us or talked to us, and she has no way of knowing that we haven't spoken to our daughter. She has no way of knowing that our daughter has been lost for years and has just come home. She was homeless and on drugs, and right before we came here tonight, we received word that she was coming home. She will be waiting for us to get back. This paper, this message, says it is time for us to heal. God is going to heal my family. He's heard my prayers. He is going to heal our family!"

She wailed. Her husband wailed. The rest of the church wailed. I apologized to God for doubting Him. On that piece of paper, I had written that they were to go home, find their daughter in her room, embrace her and forgive her. I wrote that God wanted to restore their relationship with her. That message took more faith than what I thought I had. It wasn't as simple as telling someone I liked their blouse or God saw the beauty in them. However, when I got out of my own mind and truly listened to God, He spoke. That minister and his wife went home, embraced their daughter, and started a healing process in their family. That message took me so far beyond my comfort zone that I knew it had to be from God. In fact, when I wrote it, I wasn't even certain they had a daughter.

Hearing God speak through me again has been like a homecoming with my Father. My hope for you is that you will experience what it is like to stand in the presence of your Creator without negative emotions. No matter what you have done, or what has happened to you, God wants to spend time with you. I encourage you to be a willing vessel for what He wants to do in your life. It will not be all sunshine and fairy tales. God never promised that it would be. However, we know that His plans for your life are good.

I encourage you to submerge yourself in positivity through affirmations and motivational messages. The messages I have heard through free videos on YouTube have transformed my life. From Eric Thomas, I learned not to give up, no matter what. I was inspired that there was greatness inside of me from Les Brown. I learned to face my truth from Lisa Nichols. TD Jakes taught me about healthy boundaries. And Brené Brown enlightened me on the power of vulnerability and worthiness.

Limit your time with negative people. Take note when you catch yourself being negative, and instantly transform negative thoughts into positive ones. Try changing the phrase "have to" to "get to." Try taking the words "I can't" and "I'm not" out of your vocabulary whenever possible. Start to notice when you are allowing your past to dictate your future, when you are becoming defensive, or when you are reacting negatively to a situation.

By definition, success is the accomplishment of a goal, aim, or purpose. Many people put off accomplishing their goals when they compare their qualifications to others, or when they allow other people's doubts to become their own. The limitations on your life are adopted by you alone.

Don't be afraid to allow yourself to *want* to succeed. As Les Brown so often says, "There is greatness inside of you!" You just have to believe that. You will never know the full extent of your greatness until you refine your skills. You owe it to yourself to put in the work to make your dreams come true. It is so hard to get out of bed in the morning and go through the motions of a life in which you are only playing a part.

When you find something you love so much that you would do it for free, that you would wake up at 4:00 in the morning to do it, that you would invest your time and energy into, nobody will have to tell you to do it. Get out of your own mind and set aside all the excuses to quit or reasons to fail. Your life is a direct product of your thoughts. If you just accept that you are impatient, and you don't do anything to change that characteristic, then you will continue to be impatient. If you accept that you are broken, and you don't change how you think about yourself, you will continue to be broken. If you want to create lasting change in your life and overcome your weaknesses, start with changing your thoughts.

It is going to take some time to really change the way you think. You did not develop negative habits overnight, and you will not get rid of them overnight. Be kind to yourself. Give yourself grace. Develop a plan and stick to it. Your routine will be critical to your success. Find what works for you and do it every day. When you get overwhelmed, breathe. When you fail, go back to the basics.

One of my favorite quotes comes from Brené Brown, "Worthiness doesn't have prerequisites. Here's what is truly at the heart of wholeheartedness: Worthy now, not if, not when. We're worthy of love and belonging now. Right this minute. As is."

If I may leave you with one last thing for now, it would be that you are worthy. You are worthy of the calling on your life, no matter what your past looks like. You are worthy to have a voice and to tell your story. You are worthy of friendships and healthy relationships. You are worthy of love. You are worthy of kindness. You are worthy of thoughtfulness. God created you, and you...are...good.